A Year
in the Life
of a
Bus-Traveling
Poet

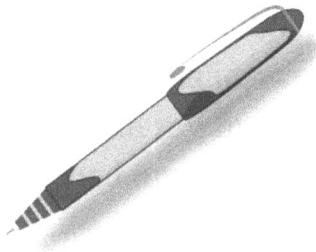

by

Marcia Mae Nelson Pedde

Acknowledgments

It is with the deepest of pleasure and appreciations galore that I acknowledge the following people: Robert MacDonald for providing me with copyright rules and regulations; Wendy Morton, "Random Acts of Poetry" poet from Sooke, British Columbia, my mentor and someone you will read more about in the pages to follow; Sylvia Plester-Silk for her continued encouragement and on-going friendship; Barb Northwood and Stefan Jonsson for just being who each of you is blessed to be; Tina Nguyen, through Twitter, who introduced me to the gogyohka style of poetry; each and every one in the Twitter world who follows me and encourages and inspires my creativity with every retweet of my verse – especially Ella; to my brother Brad who has inspired me consistently over the course of our lifetimes with his own creative passions and writing abilities; and to my life-long best friends and sisters-in-mischief, Carol, Pam and Claudia.

Dear Reader,

Please honour the blank pages within this book by gracing them with your very own poetry, prose, short stories, doodles ... any and all artistic endeavours that inspire the muse within you to create!

In Light and Laughter,

Marcia

My Husband's Wish for Me:

There,
on the bus,
on the seat,
in front of me,
a delicate, white, perfect curl
of flower petal...

Or, perhaps a tattered wing,
remainder of a fairy
too tired to fly....

Mike Nelson Pedde

Chapter One

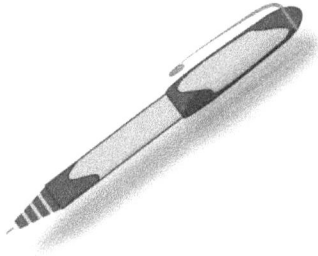

Falling in love with Victoria

*W*here do I begin this journey? At the beginning would be a typical response. Yet I choose to start mid-way through – not the tale – the year! The tale starts simply in May of 2009. The reason is an exquisite one, for me at least. I chose that particular month to take a 4-day personal retreat at Queenswood, a spiritual centre here in Victoria, British Columbia, Canada.

Much was happening in my life; I was having challenges determining my next steps and the direction they would lead me. Having ample time, yet a less than ample budget, it seemed the ideal solution.

Here's a brief write-up about this incredible oasis at the edge of the city, from its very own website http://www.queenswoodvictoria.ca/:

When you need inspiration or renewal you can find it at Queenswood.

> *Queenswood has been loved as a spiritual home-away-from home for over 40 years. Hidden away on a forested property only minutes from downtown Victoria, Queenswood is just around the corner... and yet a world away. Restore your wellness and zest for life with yoga, art, or meditation drop-in classes. Escape for a retreat, and absorb the peace of our forest sanctuary and the nearby beach. Come to Queenswood and revitalize your spirit.*

Now how could I possibly turn down such an incredible invitation? I couldn't. And I didn't!

Queenswood was the beginning place. I arrived at its doors by city bus #11, dragging along one piece of luggage. Tucked inside the wheeled suitcase were 4-days worth of clothing, personal care items, several pens and two large, empty journal books screaming out to be filled.

Did you catch that I took the public transit to get there? A very important factor for two reasons: the first being that the retreat centre was that close to town; the second was that I owned no car. I'd like to tell you that my reasons for being car-less were environmentally motivated. That would, however, not be a truth. My move to Victoria was a blend of passionate desire and financial motivation. The passionate desire had been with me since 1986. The financial motivation was a more recent challenge and a need at a deeper and different level of existence.

Relying on my own personal power when possible, I went everywhere in Victoria by foot if the distance was close enough and time permitted; by bus if time was too short or distance too great! I traveled the entire year in that fashion. I still do! Environmentally it makes sense. And the cost savings is a powerful incentive as well. Yet the sweetest reward for taking the bus is the human interaction that unfolds between individuals in closed quarters – people caring for each other, bumping into one another, needing a smile or a seat or both. There is a hub of life expressed each day within the confines of a moving space that allows 50 or more unique personalities to share a few moments together.

The story I relate to you will unfold here as it was told to my own heart – in a blend of prose and poetic formats. The poet that I am is expansive – meaning that I am open to all styles of poetic expression. Each phrase, stanza, rhyme – or lack thereof – is based on the topic, the emotion it generates and the inspiration that comes to me and through me as I write. There will be explanation, education, and playfulness throughout the book as well, for your reading pleasure!

Chapter Two

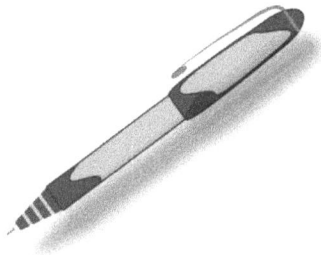

Queenswood Discovered

*a*rriving at Queenswood was an adventure all its own. Bus #11 traverses through the Uplands – a prestigious neighbourhood community of grandeur and beauty: immense properties exquisitely landscaped and bordered with mature trees lining the wide, quiet streets. This, my first journey here, was a neck-turner of an experience. I didn't know where to look, there was so much to see. To this day I take the #11 bus and get off at the very first stop within the Uplands, just to walk, gawk and dream ... of someday ...

This particular day, however, I remained on the bus till it left the Uplands, passed through the tiny, quaint village of Cadboro Bay and made a sharp left curve into a forested area and the entrance to my destination. There were two deer grazing on the grasses by the building that is the Queenswood Centre. Neither animal was the least bit agitated by my presence. The obnoxious grinding of my suitcase wheels on pavement didn't disturb them at all. As a result they granted me the joyous pleasure of stopping to rest for a moment while looking at them askance. I had been told by a wildlife biologist that it was best not to make direct eye contact with animals in their natural state. So I looked at them more furtively than straight on. I really don't think they'd have minded either way!

Welcomed at the reception desk by a delightful weekend staff member, between us we got through the paperwork and preliminary details of registering. I was treated to a relaxed, personal orientation of the facility and the wonderful options that would be available to me during my stay. With a stop in the cafeteria for tea and cookies, which we took with us back to the main reception area, we chatted at length as strangers do to make conversation. It was a pleasant interlude, yet this fine woman knew when to close the talk for the serious business of getting me ensconced in my room.

Small, yet clean, neat and fully functional, I had everything here that I would need during my retreat. The room had a single bed, neatly made with the covers already turned down (what a sweet gesture!) and fresh flowers from Queenswood's own gardens in a wee vase on the night stand. (The flowers had been picked personally, I later learned, by the very same young woman who greeted me as I first arrived.) There were fresh, crisp linens and two extra blankets laid out for the potentially cooler evenings. A desk with gooseneck lamp and chair would provide me a location to write. There was a comfy, wood-handled, padded rocker for contemplation and reading. A sink, mirror and two towel racks provided for daily personal washing and the brushing of teeth.

The shared washrooms, a mere two doors down the hall, were immaculate. My room was in the women's wing of the building, and here there were enough stalls for a convention of women. There were three shower units with a change area for each and a door to close for privacy. There was also a fair-sized room with a tub for those who preferred that mode of bathing. Closets on the wall across from the sink area were filled with a help-yourself selection of bath and hand towels, face cloths, bedding and more blankets. There was even an in-house style of accordion fold-out clothes-line to hang wet bathing suits and hand-washed items.

Back in my room, I unpacked my suitcase into the ample closet that held shelves as well. Then I brushed my teeth, got into my nightgown, opened the window and crawled into bed. I had been advised the place was relatively empty. It was, after all, the Victoria Day long weekend in May. Apparently almost everyone who worked here was away. There were no events or major planned retreats. It was very, very quiet. Listening to the breeze whispering through the tree just outside the room, I was lulled into a swift sleep.

Chapter Three

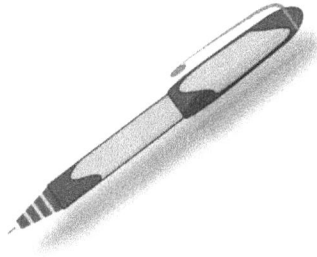

Queenswood Inspires

J awoke not knowing what time it was except by the joy of the songs expressed by the local soloists of the winged world. What a peaceful blessing to begin my day.

As I prepared for my first full day at Queenswood, I told myself I'd not read while I was here. Write, yes. I'd walk and eat, sleep, write some more, walk even more, nap if I so chose. And I also decided to talk as little as possible.

Once I was washed and dressed I went downstairs to see about breakfast and was shocked and quite delighted to find that it was just after 7 a.m. Breakfast was still an hour away! So I wandered about the building to get my bearings and happily found the library. I adore libraries. This one did not disappoint.

Sitting atop one of the many open counters was a small, soft-covered book:

Six Impossible Things Before Breakfast:
Taking Poetry Public Across Canada
by Wendy Morton

With time to spare till breakfast, I took a moment to glance through it. Seems the author flew the skies of Canada via our Canadian WestJet Airline and wrote poetry for the passengers. What an inspiring concept. Wendy was, and still is, a woman local to this area: living in Sooke just west of Greater Victoria. Holding this book of Wendy's had my mind wandering to an amazing thought – a poetry book written by me and entitled, strangely enough: A Year in the Life of a Bus-Traveling Poet.

Could I write a poetry book? Where would I start? How? By borrowing this little book from the library, enjoying the words shared and tucked neatly between the covers, then following my own bliss as inspired and incited within my soul, sparked by the tinder of Morton's talent, I knew I could do it.

Little did I know just how quickly such a dream would unfold for me!

Immediately, however, there arose an intense upheaval of fear from deep within my solar plexus. So many thoughts and questions arose – all instigated by my Inner Critic, I knew, to halt me in my tracks before even getting to the starting gate, let alone out from it. Who was I to think I could write such a book? Who would want to read it? Poetry was no longer considered the honoured skill of centuries past. With little to no demand, what publisher would take on a newcomer professing to be a poet?

Yet there was a small, child-like voice – barely audible – on the side-lines of my thoughts. I stopped to listen to it: "You can do this!" Could I really? Would I? Dare I?

"You'll start it but, like most things you've attempted to tackle in your lifetime, it'll get forgotten or nothing will come of it," the Inner Critic interjected.

I knew it was fear that had reared its ugly presence within me. Was I experiencing fear of failure? Fear of success? Maybe it was a flighty vision – not worthy of more than a pipe dream.

Or, would my initial passion for such a concept stay with me through to the completion of realizing such a possibility? Was that tiny voice worth paying attention to?

How would I know the answers to any of these queries unless I gave this a try? Might it be that simple? This was my first morning here at Queenswood. I came here to open myself up to possibilities. Could the solution be that easy? I came seeking answers. Were the answers waiting within these walls all this time?

I signed for the Morton book and tucked it in with my writing materials as I headed down the hall to the dining area.

****

There were very few people at breakfast. I gathered the foods I wanted from the wide selection of options, nestled myself at a window table and enjoyed my first retreat meal. It was delicious.

Sipping at my coffee, I was watching the activities of the swallows outside the expansive dining hall window when this inspiration struck:

Swallows
with their aerodynamic wing tips
and easy glide,
suddenly dart
with amazing
mobility,
to grace the still air
decorating the tranquil beauty
of the new day.

I had come seeking answers. Were the answers waiting within these walls all this time? It seems that they were, and I was open enough to hear them!

******

Less than a half hour later, more poetry was streaming from my pen:

From the Cafeteria Window

Still as a naturalist's painting
Each leaf perfect
Tones and shades and hues
Of greens exquisitely blended.
Rose and reds and russets
Complimenting, contrasting, clashing
Like the visual cacophony
Of a world-renowned symphony
Its first day of rehearsal.
The eye wants to seek out,
To stroke every texture.
The awe, the majesty
Is spellbinding
Until ...
Into the landscape
On as yet unsure but gentle foot
Steps the gangly grace
Of a newly born fawn.
The stillness of the scene
Is broken by the curious exploration
Of innocence
And yet ...
There is now incredible quiet
Within the observer
Not daring to move a muscle
To breathe
Or to take the chance of
A single blink breaking
The perfection of this moment,
This snapshot of time
As still as a naturalist's painting.

I lay down for a nap after writing the previous poem. How is it someone could need more sleep after having had a good night's rest?

22

Yet I slept soundly. The dreams were powerful. Everyone in the dream was either one of the needy or someone who could help. I remember a glimmer of being one who helped – by lying with a very young boy in a hospital-like atmosphere. My wrapping him in my arms, cuddling him as he slept, allowed him the comfort of feeling loved and permitted him the sleep and rest he needed.

When I got downstairs, I was agog at the time: I had slept a full three hours! I obviously needed that nap and the journey into the dreamtime. Spiritual places do that for me.

I was surprised at how hungry I was. Lunch was on, so I enjoyed another delicious meal; relaxing yet again over my coffee and the great view of the lawns and lush gardens. Sadly, no poems were hollering to be heard just then.

Having placed my dishes in the clean-up area, I headed back up to my assigned room. My window overlooked a rather complex labyrinth, the symbol of which was part of the Queenswood logo. The thought initially crossed my mind to walk the maze below, yet before I could take action on that option, Wendy Morton's wee book caught my attention. The title she chose for it came from the "Queen of Hearts" character in the book **Alice in Wonderland**. The queen says that she spends at least a half hour every day believing in impossible things ... even as many as "six impossible things before breakfast". To me this was inspiring.

Six impossible things: how would 'impossible' translate into my existence? How might I define, delineate and reveal impossible into *probable* in my life? What would *probable* look like? What courage would I need to make it happen? What joyous tomfoolery could I, would I, pursue to create the fulfillment of a dream?

****

Just past lunch, more creativity bubbled up from within:

Inspiration requires seven simple steps.
The opening of each of the six senses
And the linking of each,
One to the other.
Woven and interwoven,
Vein and artery,
Into a tapestry of breathtaking beauty
Each stitch
The beating of my heart.

Then another:

The Answer to my Prayer

Lying on my bed attempting to nap
Looking for a dream to inspire an action
Waiting to know the action to take
To inspire the dream.

Then outside my window singing its heart out to me
Comes the melodious message simple and true
The herald of a robin.
Listen carefully ... listen, do ...

"Tell it. Tell it.
Read it. Tell it.
Write it. Read it.
Poet, do!"

The song of the Robin will now never be heard
Without knowing the truth of its encouraging word.

For 60 plus years of my earth walk, I have listened to the call of the robin. Heralding in the spring, the robin welcomes the dawn of each new day, and takes no vacation till departing in the autumn – when our Canadian leaves fall. Yet till this day, I had never understood its language.

****

25

Sauntering through Queenswood's halls, I wound my way up and down various sets of stairs more for the exercise than any specific destination. Thinking it might be close to dinner, I headed back to the entrance of this peaceful facility to discern the time. This particular location was the only place that had a clock. Yet being unaware of the time did not hinder my progress through this lovely day.

Speaking of lovely days, this one had the added bonus of a languorously refreshing spring rain and the creation of a poem to commemorate it:

Celebrate the rain!
Wash the dust from the body
Drop by drop.
Quench the thirst.
Renew the blood.
Energize the cells.
Drop by precious drop.
Blessings be.
Celebrate the rain!

******

The dear woman who registered me here at Queenswood last evening stopped by my room. She had just gotten back from seeing the movie Star Trek – the Prequel. Seems she loved it as much as I did. We had both learned they might be showing it at the massive IMAX theatre here in Victoria. We laughed about the fact that we'd likely see each other there ... several times!

Hearing my own voice chatting with her, I realized that was the first time I had spoken all day – and with laughter. How wonderful!

Before bedtime, I chose to walk through the facility once more. I stopped near one particular section that I had not taken time to admire before now.

It was still raining, and listening to both the raindrops plopping on the leaves and on the ground outside and the waterfall bubbling in the huge vase close behind me where I stood ... the energy and flow of water seemed a powerful element – soothing to the soul.

Those thoughts triggered another verse:

Raindrops on pavement through window before me
Waterfall dripping in huge vase behind me
The energy and flow of water
As powerful element
Is soothing to the soul.

Incredible how simple it can be to transfer a thought into poetry. This particular poem I have since learned has a specific name. It is one of the Japanese haiku styles of poetry called a *tanka*: five lines; the first three lines and last three lines each capable of standing alone.

******

That night, as I closed my eyes to sleep, offering my appreciations to the Divine for the most incredible and inspiring of days, I realized that I had written six poems. Six! Just like "six impossible things ..." Blessings be! Queenswood certainly does inspire!

27

Chapter Four

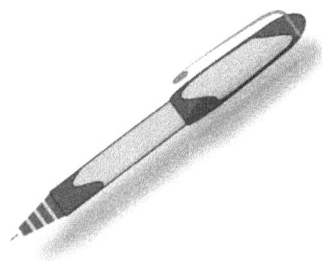

Day Two

*W*aking on day two to the morning call of the birds rather than the blaring of an alarm, I stretched languorously, took a few deep breaths and then crawled out from under the bed covers. There was no clock in my room and not having one of my own – watches never work properly on me; neither wind-up nor digital – I had no idea what time it was. Feeling only slightly hungry, I assumed there would be enough time to wash up and dress at a leisurely pace – which is exactly what I did.

Once my ablutions were complete, I sauntered down to the front welcoming area with my journal book and pen in hand. I was amazed to discover it was only 6:40 a.m.! The initial shock – I am normally not an early riser – was replaced with delight as it seemed I had the building to myself for a while still and I found a quiet corner with a comfy chair, into which I happily nestled and wrote copiously into my journal book.

My writing reflected back to the previous evening's unfolding: back in my room by 7 p.m.; wrote a wee bit; read a bit from Wendy Morton's book; then hopped into bed. Even having had a nap during the day, I was tired. Yet once I got into bed and the lights were out, suddenly I got an idea to write a poem for the woman who welcomed me to Queenswood. It was such fun to do! Once completed – and in its original state with no edits or alterations – I snuggled once more under the blankets. Almost relaxed enough to doze off, another poem popped into my head. Up I got to write another full poem with no corrections required. Finally the third attempt to sleep was effective and dreamless right through till the birds began to celebrate the arrival of my second day here.

With breakfast still a few minutes away, my mind wandered to places and thoughts unknown, while looking out the picture window. Movement outside brought me back from wherever my mind had taken me. A deer, a doe, was sauntering her way across the lawn –

trusting, safe, knowing she had no need for concern, no risk to her life or her journey.

The arrival of this beautiful creature seemed a suitable analogy for my own search for such peace and safety. I had taken some pretty wild journeys the past several years. Many I had been grateful for. Some I regretted deeply. Each experience had crafted and defined my life as it now existed. For this I was predominantly appreciative. And yet ...

A sudden surge of fear filled me once again. There was a reason I was here at Queenswood. On some level I knew I needed to be open to growth and possibility. I just had no idea what shape any of this might take; what it might look like, taste like, feel like. I knew there was something major missing – a piece of the puzzle of my life – and either it was because the piece was not on the table yet, so to speak, or because I was just not seeing it in amongst all the other pieces scattered about!

Even if I found this one puzzle piece, would I have the courage to actually seek out the ideal spot for it to go, the place in my life that it could fit into perfectly in order to complete my life's purpose?

My mind abandoned me once again to thoughts it was unwilling to share or preferred not to reveal. When I recognized that fact I also realized that the deer had wandered off in search of tasty morsels elsewhere. She had come, whether or not she was aware of her role, to inspire me to deep contemplation. I gave a quick word of thanks for her presence and her gift. Then I headed off for breakfast.

Later that morning I was appreciating the fact that I was truly enjoying writing poetry. Over the years – since I was a child, actually – I have been known to record a verse or two. Yet I always saw myself more as a novelist or short story writer. The novels seemed elusive – with many of them having been started and (as was typical of me) never finished. I had quite a lovely collection of short stories that I was proud of – though none had ever been published other than one children's tale posted on a friend's website.

The nice thing I was finding out about the poetry these past two days was the ease of starting and finishing a complete thought, an idea, or an inspiration from beginning to end in a matter of a few stanzas. With the completion of each poem I could then move on to something else. To write a book requires – actually demands – more of me. So the question arose: which is more reflective of me and what I need to do to express myself, to create through myself and be wholly who I truly am?

I realized that I loved the way I was feeling just thinking about this. I had a sense of excitement for myself, not knowing what was about to arise, yet knowing that something special was, in fact, about to happen. I felt ready, willing and open to the joy of ideas, the magic of words and phrases and the marvel of whatever *it* was that was all coming together for me. Thoughts of the majesty of divine (maybe even Divine) intervention filled me with awe. The amazement of such potential, of the creativity and the wonder at whatever outcome might arrive on my doorstep, absolutely thrilled me to pieces!

Then fear reared its ugly head once more. Incredibly, I had the courage to tell it to take a hike! I liked the way my body felt: enthusiastic, hopeful, encouraged, and completely, wonderfully right.

Yet I did ask myself – and my Self – where I intended to take things from here? Was this to be an occasional, momentary, once-in-a-while hobby? Or should I, could I, would I take it further?

When no answers were forthcoming, I decided to let it go – just for now – to trust that I was at Queenswood for a reason and that reason would be revealed in its own and perfect time. I acknowledged to my Self that I merely needed to remain open and ready to receive any beautiful gems as they presented themselves over the course of the next few days.

Chapter Five

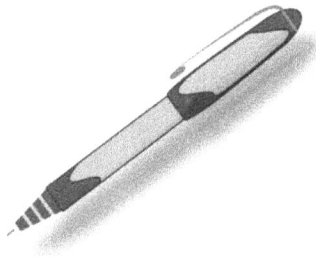

The Pantoum

Since I am always happy to add to my poetic abilities, I was delighted to discover a new poetry style. In Wendy's book (definitely a worth read!), she describes a style of poetry I'd never heard of before – the Pantoum. It is a French form of poetry with a rather complex pattern of line repetition.

Here's the functional intricacy: Start with a 4-line stanza.

1.
2.
3.
4.

Then when you go to write the second 4-line stanza, repeat two of the lines written in the first stanza:

2.
5.
4.
6.

Same thing with the 3rd stanza. Repeat two of the lines in the second stanza

5.
7.
6.
8.

And so on…finishing up with the very last line of your poem being the same as the first line of it.

7.
9.
8.
10.

9.
3.
10.
1.

Here's an example from one of my own – in fact, my very first ever – Pantoum!

1. **Each day a new start**
2. **A fresh new beginning**
3. **A chance to improve**
4. **To aim for perfection.**

2. **A fresh new beginning**
5. **A pure white, clean slate**
4. **To aim for perfection**
6. **As I move through my day.**

5. **A pure white, clean slate**
7. **That demands being filled**
6. **As I move through my day**
8. **Creative endeavours.**

7. **That demands being filled**
9. **To the fullest, the best**
8. **Creative endeavours**
10. **Gentle heart, soft smile.**

9. **To the fullest, the best**
3. **A chance to improve**
10. **Gentle heart, soft smile**
1. **Each day a new start.**

Since then I've found myself using the Pantoum style any time I want to delve deeper into a concept. I've used it to expand ideas, to open myself up when blocked about something, and to more fully explore a fabulous emotional response to a person or situation. Basically, when I want to understand my own self better, I take a thought or idea and 'Pantoum' it!

Should you feel inclined to try the style yourself, do so! I heartily encourage it!

Try it out here:

(TITLE)

1. _____
2. _____
3. _____
4. _____

2. _____
5. _____
4. _____
6. _____

5. _____
7. _____
6. _____
8. _____

7. _____
9. _____
8. _____
10. _____

9. _____
3. _____
10. _____
1. _____

Chapter Six

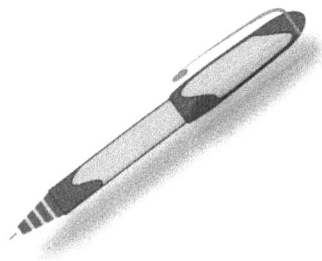

Guidance

*M*y personal retreat time at Queenswood was intentionally a search for inner guidance. Guidance, I have learned over the years, comes in many guises. Mine, during my short stay at this blessed place, happened to come in a delightful package – one of the Sisters of St. Anne. As a service offered to Queenswood guests, counselling can be made available. Since this was my journey, I was not surprised that the appropriate someone had the time to see me. What an incredibly revealing experience this was.

Let me first set the stage for you as to where my head and my heart were at before I attended my first appointment – my pre-appointment thoughts, if you will. I was very nervous. Not Catholic (or religious at all, for that matter), I do have a strong spiritual belief but feared those beliefs might not hold me in a strong enough stead to talk to, and share myself with, a Sister of any religion! So, I thought it best to preset the stage and grant myself some peace before I walked in to see this woman. Since I wrote out my thoughts, I quote them to you here:

> *"Self, be open to hearing and receiving all that I need to hear and to know; all that will allow me to become stronger, wiser, better, happier, more me. Let me share that which will reveal my inner self in ways to bring this consultation to a height of spiritual guidance that inspires the best in me. Help me to step through the fear and into trust and faith – with confidence and joy and inner beauty."*

Though the actual sessions (and there were two over as many days, an hour each) will not be discussed here due to their very personal nature, I will say that the overall revelations and the AHA moments were profound.

I had hoped that there might be a poem forthcoming from the revelations of the first session, yet that did not happen. Rather, I went for a much-needed walk to clear my head afterward.

Spring in Victoria is an amazing and vibrant time of year. Everything comes to life almost overnight. One moment a wee bit of green can be seen to pop up through the soil and peak out from in amongst browned patches. A mere few days later a profusion of lushness hides all of last season's old growth. Walking through the woods that surround Queenswood, I felt myself to be as the new and succulent vegetation, reaching out to the sun for sustenance and life itself.

Yet I also had a sense within me of laughter bubbling to the surface. What a delicious and exhilarating feeling! As I continued to walk along the pathways, I observed a cluster of fiddleheads – the delectable precursors to the wood ferns they would soon become. Fiddleheads are a delicacy when prepared with the guided hand of a qualified chef. Thinking this thought I got suddenly giddy and the following poem popped into my mind:

Fiddleheads, Fiddleheads
Opening up
Swirling, still furling
Upon you I'll sup.
A fern you will be
If I leave you behind ...
But I'll eat you with dinner.
I hope you don't mind.

Laughter, like singing, brings a natural breathing rhythm to the body – deep, resonant, healing. I laughed my way back to my room!

Chapter Seven

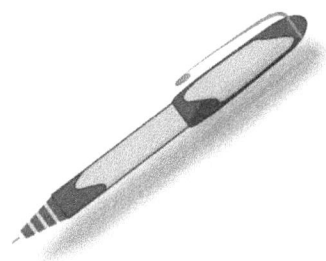

Reflecting Back

*F*or this one chapter I felt it appropriate to take a step back into the past – my past. There is no need for you to know about my life prior to this moment in time. Yet I do want you to have a sense of the passion and the gift – the talent – that came with the package I chose to be born within.

Poetry is, was and shall always be my driving force. Up to this point in my life, the gift was a hobby. It was fun. Poetry and verse allowed me to express the world around me in ways that words spoken could never reveal. One did not speak in verse to twenty-first century habitants.

Most of what I recorded I kept. Over the years there have been certain poems that clearly expressed my life, my beliefs, my drives and passions at that time, as a snapshot might. I thought to include a sample, or microcosmic collection if you will, of the works that in their own fashion describe my life's unfolding.

Here for you, then, is some of that collection:

Ode to Joy

The rippling of a summer breeze

brought to vibrating life

in the melodic flow of a silken scarf

held proudly high

by the hands of an innocent child.

Wordsmithing

The crafting of words is an art
A creation of thought onto paper
Into a turn of phrase
Shaped by tongue and mouth
A specialized form of communication
With self and others.

As potter shapes the clay
And painter holds a brush
So too the wordsmith
Molds and transforms
Letter and sound from concept
To visual or audible perception
Open to the interpretation of the recipient.

Me as wordsmith
How did this unfold?
Crafted in the depth of mind
To keep away the cold.
Thoughts to banish feelings
Better left alone
To draw the warmth of people near
To push away the moan
Within my heart.

MAGIC

Magic is around every corner
Marvel in every face
Mischief in every encounter
Majesty in each precious place.

Awe fills the senses with wonder
Artistic creations abound
And the joy, the peace through creating
Awakens the gifts needing found.

Great is the calm of creation
Gifts crying out for release
Granted through cooperation
Gently enticing the peace.

Into the heart goes the talent
Into the mind and the soul
Inspiration is drawn from the selfhood
Intuition is drawn from the whole.

Crafting the art through expression
Concocted with paper and pen
Certain of nothing 'cept passion till
Completed. Ah, magic again!

No title – not yet finished….

"What do I want?" I ask myself
As the sun rises over the hill.
So much beauty within my life
What more would I will?

Mountains as far as the eye can see
Birds of every feather
Skies so clear and clouds unique
And incredibly perfect weather.

A job with people I adore
Doing things I like
And especially loving and being loved
By my wonderful husband Mike!

I reside in a home that shelters me.
There is a bed on which to rest
There are funds for food to fill my face
With all of nature's best.

The clothes upon my person
Are clean and in good repair
My body is washed and nourished
And I have shampoo for my hair.

I am happy with my beingness
With my marriage and my friends
I enjoy my life, my work, my skills
The pleasures never end.

Yet....this home does not belong to me
No car do I possess
The money in my wallet
Is for things I need – no less.

The extras that I choose to have
Though some I grab in greed
Seem to elude my having them
Not even for my need.

And as I write these aching words
My energy recedes
The jubilance I felt at first
No longer does its deed.

Before I head to work again
Fulfilling a belief
I look into a clear blue sky
And touch a living leaf.

I take the time to nourish me
My soul, my very being
Allowing me to walk my talk
Open to inner seeing.

For who I am is linked in love
To all of my creation....
The joyous feel of my intent
Enhances my elation.

Emotions

Emotions raw and red and angry
Fear of fallow yellow freezing action
Marble motion stone cold
Thawed with a tear
Broken apart by the crack of a smile
A flaw of the heart
The seed of love
Aggressive in its drive
To touch the sun
Sadness' black cloud
Shrouds the perception
Smothers the jubilation
Stifles the spontaneity of life
Blinded.
No thing of value
Is recognized by its true
Lightness of being
The complexity, the kaleidoscope
Of shifting emotions
Presents such altered
Fractured responses
With a simple turn of fancy.
A whole new compilation of
Flavourful tidbits
Tantalize the senses
Luscious choices to uplift and nourish
Every aspect of self
The gentlest of smiles forms from deep within
And cracks the stone.

Results

Things will turn out well.

They always do.

Fears

Insecurities are the stuff
Of my own trepidations
My 'not wanted' creations.

Zzzzzzs

I'm going to catch

some Zzzzzzs

to put me at ease

as I begin my day.

I'm a sleep junky.

Ancient Wisdom

I am woman

Old and stooped

Wise and wizened

Eyes sparkling crystal.

I reach out to encompass

Tree and blossom

Groundhog and owl

Horse and hawk.

I speak to brook and mountain.

I am woman.

I embody power

I exude passion

My need extends beyond self

to life itself

And love of all around me.

Senses

I smell the scent
And in my mind's eye
I am there.
Fond memories revealed
In instant replay –
Pine camping,
Lavender grandmother,
Coconut sandy shores.
Sounds too
And 3D effects
Pull immediate smiles
From inner recall
To outer persona.

Early Morning Heartbeat

To arise before the sun,

To sing my heart's song

Before a single bird takes flight,

To be at peace within myself

Is the joy of life.

Blank Page

A blank page needs purpose.

Chapter Eight

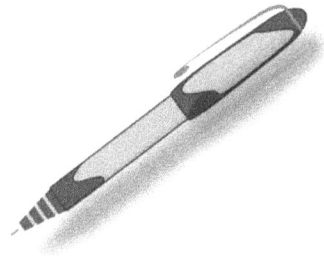

Authority

*S*ister, who remains nameless for privacy, got me chatting about a wide range of topics. One that surfaced with passion from within me was my writing. That didn't surprise me in the least. Yet what became evident for the very first time was my identity with the title word of 'author'. It seemed I had not taken time to own this gift and the responsibility that accompanied it.

I spent a lifetime deferring to those in authority 'over' me – parents, teachers, doctors, clergy, managers – each had always held the power. Their views, their words, their directives had always held more value, more demand, than my own.

Sister sweetly suggested I rephrase those two sentences in order to shift the control. I had always **allowed** each to hold the power over me. I had **permitted** their values to hold more influence in my life than the influence of my very own values. Major shift in focus!

No one need have power over me any longer. They never did. I had never granted myself permission to recognize the simplicity of what had always been right in front of me.

From that incredible eye-opening recognition, it was suggested that I consider allowing an opening to my own inner 'authority'. Should I choose to take on the active role as an author, I would be granting myself permission to be, and to provide, my own 'authority' from which I would gain guidance and inspiration. Proudly opening to my own inner 'authority' rightly placed me in a solid stance to accept my own wisdom and value – and to have something of substance to offer each reader of my works. Was I ready?

Chapter Nine

Authenticity

*W*as I ready? Was I ready to take on authority and responsibility? Was I ready to accept guidance and open myself up to the recognition of my own innate wisdom, value and the blessing of divine inspiration? That certainly was a tall order for someone who had learned, from a lifetime of societal conditioning, that it was inappropriate to speak up. And yet, it felt so right.

The discussion with Sister came to a very powerful and positive close that first day. She offered that we could meet again the same time the very next day. Would I find that suitable? I took a moment to look inside and the answer was a resounding YES. So we made the appointment, and went our separate ways after sharing a brief, and sincere, hug.

I wandered the grounds after the appointment and prior to dinner. There was so much to think about and so much more that was surfacing as emotion. Fear, certainly. Yet there was a sense of eagerness making itself known within me.

Eagerness – I like that word. I liked the sensation of it roaming around inside me, resonating in my mind and my solar plexus. I was eager for change. I was eager for new beginnings. I was eager for the opportunity to see what I could do if I put my mind to something I cared deeply and passionately about accomplishing. Could I do it? Could I truly become a writer? Did I love writing enough to be a writer whether or not I was paid to write?

What would happen if I did step into that potential role? How would it all unfold? Who would I become? Sister had walked me through a meditation during our session. I found peace in that experience. So, I took a moment to go back into that quiet space within myself to see what answers might come to me. The result seemed less effective than when I was guided earlier: less effective, that is, until I opened my inner ears to hear a word that was trying to be heard and understood.

I came back from that gentle place with an additional concept to mull over – authenticity. Authority and authenticity – both were demanding attention, autonomy, and acceptance within me. Hmmm ... it seemed like I was starting with the very first letter of the alphabet – A – for my inner lessons on becoming truly my Self.

Someone once asked me if I knew of anything that I would do even if I never got paid to do it? Always the answer came through loud and clear – I would write no matter what! This then, they said, was my PASSION (their emphasis). My passion is also my life's purpose. Dare I step into the gift and claim my right to it?

By the time I fell exhausted into the small single bed, I knew the answer to be a very confident affirmative. There was a fire burning within me that I had never acknowledged before that day. It had been a healthy stoked flame within me as a child – that much I knew so very clearly. Yet as I matured into adulthood, the flames had receded – most of them doused with the cold waters of reality and ridicule – to mere embers on the verge of being extinguished. My session with Sister had brought those embers back to a hearty blaze once again!

Chapter Ten

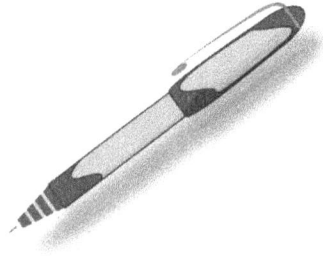

Gratitude

*S*o much had happened during my day that I was too excited to sleep. Emotions were racing within me in a playful, gleeful manner. There were concepts craving acknowledgement. Probabilities and possibilities were vying for attention. And fear, the tool of the unaware adult, was trying to holler out a warning to them all. Fortunately fear's voice was being drowned out by the eagerness of my resurrected childhood passions.

So many voices wanted to speak. I grabbed the one most calming message coming through – my deep appreciation for Sister. Here's what I wrote:

Thank you, Sister
For the gift of your ears.
You heard what I shared
And what went unspoken.

Thank you, Sister
For the gift of your gentleness
That lay its softness
Upon my heart that I may heal.

Thank you, Sister
For the gift of your insight,
Your wisdom, your counsel,
All received with deepest appreciation.

Thank you for the blessed gift of you,
Your steadfast guidance grounding
As I went in search of, and found,
Me.

What a pleasure to express my gratitude on paper. I proudly wrote that poem formally onto a delightfully decorated note card that I slipped smoothly into its matching envelope to present to Sister the next day. Only then was I able to settle enough to sleep.

Chapter Eleven

Expansion

*S*ettle and sleep I did, yet I awoke twice through the night: once to the sound of what I thought to be thunder, though there was no rain; the other from a dream that I did not record and no longer recall.

Still, I was awake, showered, dressed and down for breakfast with twenty minutes yet to wait. I took the time to sit at the huge picture window in the library watching the deer nibbling at the grasses. So calm they were, so unafraid. Or is it that they trust?

My appointment with Sister this second day added a richer depth and broader scope to what we had begun the day prior: expanding on the concept of authority. She granted me a safe place to share, to open up, and to be me, fully and completely.

What we did at first was a meditation. Different from the previous day, Sister based this one on something I had said the day before – that I felt I was missing roots. I have moved much in my life: more than most – over 35 times. In all that time there has not been a place to call home till I chose to move here to Victoria, and I'm still a fresh transplant to this fair city.

The meditation started with the same relaxation techniques. Then I was guided to sit by a tree of my choosing, one that would instill a sense of comfort or trust or both. I envisioned the tree to be a very old, very wise Grandmother Oak tree; one I used to visit every time I traveled to Canada's capital city of Ottawa. Often I would 'go' to her during meditation. Yet never had I experienced what was about to occur ...

Roots from the oak moved gently up from the earth – undulating out from the soil at the same diameter as the tips of the outer branches of the tree herself. The roots then, with my permission, arose up into my being. Now this may sound creepy (pun intentional) to some of you, but it was an incredible spiritual event for me.

71

In my head I heard ever so clearly, "These are your roots!" The feelings overwhelmed me to the point of tears – though I may not have a 'home', I always have roots. Wherever I am, I am rooted, grounded, solid, loved, nourished, nurtured, and supported.

What a way to begin our second day together! Any hesitation I may have had as to what I could possibly discuss for another hour and why I might want to do so vanished right from the start!

In addition to honouring the 'author' in me, in addition to recognizing and listening to and following through on my own wisdoms surfacing from the 'authority' of my own being, Sister encouraged me to grant myself permission to 'authorize' that wisdom and its expression out into the world.

It became significant for me on that day to begin to authorize my talents, my writings, my laughter, my hugs, and my poems to be given freely, without restriction. No holding back. Trust my inner voice. Do not look outside myself for approval, validation or my next steps. Know what my next steps are by listening to my inner 'authority' and by 'authorizing' action based on what was right for me as guided by me – the author of my own journey.

With Sister to guide me, I laughed, I cried, I giggled and shared. My eyes, I know, got big as saucers and I heard myself saying over and over and over again – WoW! There was confirmation after confirmation coming at me, encouraging and enticing me, to listen to and to follow through into action the counsel of my inner 'author'. I felt so at peace, so happy, so eager, and so blessed.

Sister was, for me, such a dear, sweet, caring, nurturing, supportive woman and an incredible gift to me. I carry her beauty in my expanded heart even now.

Following our session, the giving and receiving of hugs once again, and my gift to her of the poem I wrote for her, I headed out for an afternoon walk. I had to stop to write another poem that surfaced within my being. Pantoum-style seemed appropriate for this poem. (Note: Refer back to Chapter 5 for the unique repetitious line-use technique applied here):

The Freedom to Be

The freedom to be me
Starts from within my heart
Is spoken by my own authority
My own divine counsellor.

Starts from within my heart
Spreads to all of my being
My own divine counsellor
Is wise beyond my ken.

Spreads to all of my being
From inner knowing to outer showing
Is wise beyond my ken
Yet with trust is known to me.

From inner knowing to outer showing
Expressed out to the physical
Yet with trust is known to me
If I but stop to listen.

Expressed out to the physical
Is spoken by my own authority
If I but stop to listen to
The freedom to be me.

Chapter Twelve

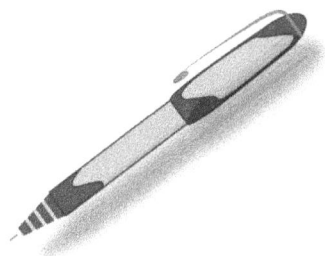

Gifts of Poems

*L*ater that same day, the third of only four days here at Queenswood, I spent time writing poems for people I had met: folks who had impressed me with a smile or a comment or had offered to assist me in some fashion or who shared a personal story with me.

I took one particular aspect of our communication with each other and made it noteworthy enough to write it up into a poem. For example: Judy (not her real name) who, like myself, was a guest and on a personal retreat, had just arrived and was celebrating a very special birthday. Her retreat was a gift to herself from herself. Nice gift! Judy's poem I recorded in my neatest script on a pretty card and popped it into an envelope. I put the card on the dining table I knew she would sit at over her breakfast in the morning.

I was delighted to be present when Judy came down that morning. I watched her as she found, opened and read the contents. I was also blessed to get a terrific hug from her afterwards!

Here is Judy's poem to give you an example of what I was moved to write. I trust it will help you to see the simplicity of topic, yet the way something like that can be pulled together into poetic format:

Good morning, Judy, birthday girl! Enjoy your gift to you.
Cherish every moment here and to yourself be true.
May the gentle loving quiet softly hold you in its hand.
And when you leave these hallowed halls may you be cushioned
where you land.
Each day within the coming year may blessings overflow
For every dream shall be fulfilled in ways you've yet to know!

I wrote and gave personalized, handwritten poems to several people that day: the receptionist, a volunteer, another of the Sisters, the program director of the facility, and one of the cooks. I was on a roll and the poems were all as varied in length and style as were the individuals they were written for and about. I was energized! And the more I wrote, the more energizing the experience became!

This was to be my last night here. I made sure to allow myself sufficient time to have dinner, pack and then go for an evening walk. The sun was setting, inspiring another poem to arise. The style of this poem I didn't know at the time (but have since learned) is a type of haiku called the gogyohka. You'll learn more about it (including how to pronounce it) in Chapter 36:

Sunset symphony
scents of cedar
and fresh mown grass
titillate the senses
I'm smiling!

The sounds and scents were heady and truly worth drenching myself in them! A mixed bag of emotions surfaced during my walk. Scents and aromas tend to do that for me – bring feelings forward to be observed, examined.

Chapter Thirteen

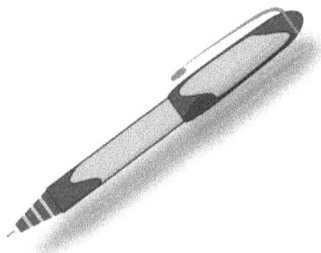

The Last Hours

*T*he night passed with a dreamless sleep. The birds were their ever-efficient selves, providing fabulous alarm service as my wake-up call. This was to be my last day of retreat here at Queenswood. It was a beautiful, fresh, sunshiny morning.

With my bags packed and the room tidied, I scooted down to the library – a regular spot during my time here – to watch the deer on their morning feeding rounds. This vantage point was the ideal place from which to observe them.

Knowing I was to leave this amazing place, my emotions were at the surface: a mixture of highs and lows, of elation and trepidation. At least the trepidation felt one notch less troublesome than fear would have been.

I found myself breathing deeply. I took one large breath and repeated the last line of one of my Pantoum poems from the past few days: Gentle heart, soft smile (*refer back to page 38*). I breathed the words into my being, like a mantra: gentle heart as I inhaled; soft smile as I exhaled. I began to feel the smile, not merely on my lips, but now also within my cells. It felt wonderful.

Once a sense of balance returned, I headed down for my last Queenswood meal. As always, it was scrumptious. Stayed – or should I say stalled – over another coffee: attempting to waylay the inevitable. However ...

I popped back down to the library after breakfast to return the Morton book. **Six Impossible Things Before Breakfast** by Wendy Morton: a small book, big on gifts. Size-wise it may be tiny, yet the content was precisely what I needed to kick-start my own journey to places the wings of an airplane could never take me – deeply within myself.

The synchronicity between the two of us, Wendy Morton and me, is quite remarkable: both of us in our 60s; both having written poetry all our lives; both having taken a personal retreat (Queenswood for me and Glenairley for Wendy) – yet both within Victoria. Fascinatingly similar ... shall my life move in such a powerful and dramatic direction as hers?

Have I the courage to write poems for people wherever I go – giving them the gift of those poems before I leave their presence? Have I the courage to write my books; to step forward with confidence into a future of my dreams and my creations? I have, if I choose to allow it.

There was one last thing I needed to accomplish before I made my final departure from these hallowed halls to journey into my future: take a walk through the labyrinth. From my room it looked to be an easy process ambling along the maze to the center. Before I headed into the predesigned pattern, I gave some meditative thought as to an intention for this walk: to receive whatever additional gifts I was willing to allow myself on the next stage of my life's adventures.

Taking my time, I proceeded with slow and deliberate steps. I found myself experiencing a going within. The closer I got to the center of the maze, the deeper the sense of separation I felt from the world around me. By the time I reached the middle, it was as though I had walked to the very core of my own soul. I can't describe it any more precisely than that.

I stood in that very spot for what could have been a moment or an hour. As I stood, I cried. Wrenching sobs erupted from me – one right after another, and another, and still more. I held nothing back. I released the tears, and the negative emotions that attached themselves to every drop. I opened up the floodgates to make room for potential growth. I sucked in air as I gulped between gasps. There was an ebb and flow; a give and take; a letting go of negative and an opening up to the positive. There was hope.

What was left was the sense of the most amazing peace I have ever known. Everything – absolutely everything – was perfect in my world in that very moment.

Chapter Fourteen

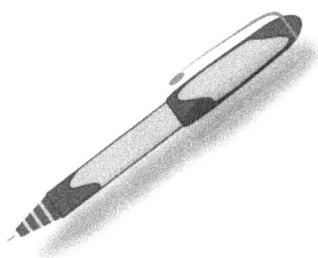

A New Beginning

*B*ag, baggage and books, I bussed my way back to my bachelor apartment. Heading north, and slightly west from Queenswood, the Victoria Transit chauffeur took us on a scenic tour of the expansive student, and rabbit, populated University of Victoria (UVic) campus. One transfer and twenty-eight minutes later, I was able to unload my luggage and put the kettle on for a tea.

Now what?

Seemed a nap was in order as I closed my eyes for just a moment while I waited for the tea to steep. Two hours later ...

I chuckled to myself when I realized the time. And that's when this next Pantoum poem came rushing at me. Fortunately I always keep my journal book handy and didn't have to go rummaging about to find something to write in, or with:

Decisions, Decisions

The prime decision
I need to make
Before the month is out
Is open for debate

I need to make
A major choice
It's open for debate
Which way I go

A major choice
Is do I move?
Which way to go?
The Bed and Breakfast?

Is do I move
The right choice now?
The Bed and Breakfast
It sounds exciting

The right choice now
Before the month is out
It sounds exciting
The prime decision

Decisions: that was to be the next phase of my journey. Stay or go. Stay put where I was or accept the challenge that was dropped in my lap before I left for my retreat. The energy that I felt with the writing of the Pantoum – a terrific conundrum-buster of an activity – clearly indicated I would be leaving this little place.

Two strikingly powerful things happened before that same day ended: both were perfect expressions of creative intention and divine intervention. The phone rang. The woman with whom I had interviewed before I left for my retreat at Queenswood called to offer me the live-in position as assistant at her bed and breakfast over the summer and until Thanksgiving in October. The position was to begin the first week of June if I was interested. I accepted.

Moments later, the phone rang again. My youngest son needed a place to stay for a few months during the summer starting June first while he completed his BA at Royal Roads University here in Victoria.

"How about staying at my place?" I readily offered.

****

One more Pantoum came floating by before I fell asleep:

A Successful Person

I am trying to be
Everything I have heard
Makes a successful person
A successful person.

Everything I have heard
Added to all that I am
A successful person
In my own right.

Added to all that I am
How can being other than I am
In my own right
Make me happy?

How can being other than I am
A powerful, talented woman
Make me happy?
Be myself.

A powerful, talented woman
Makes a successful person.
Be the 'myself'
I am trying to be.

Chapter Fifteen

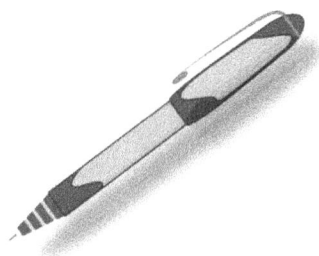

Just For Fun

**Dr. Babbitt
drives a Rabbit
out of habit,
mostly.**

Poetry is such fun! The fact that my mind works in weird and wacky ways certainly helps.

Chapter Sixteen

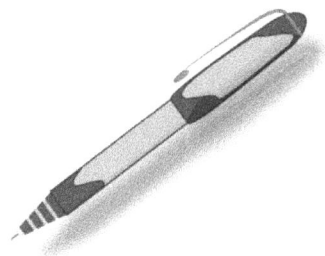

Victoria's Word

*J*n Elizabeth Gilbert's wonderful book, **Eat Pray Love**, she has a conversation with a friend about why Rome is a beautiful city, yet she feels it is not 'her' city. Her friend says that each city, and each person, has a word to describe them, and if your word and the city's word don't match, you'll never be comfortable there:

> *He said, "Don't you know that the secret to understanding a city and its people is to learn – what is the word on the street?"*
>
> *Then he went on to explain [...] that every city has a single word that defines it, that identifies most people who live there. If you could read people's thoughts as they were passing you on the streets of any given place, you would discover that most of them are thinking the same thought. Whatever that majority thought might be – that is the word of the city. And if your personal word does not match the word of the city, then you don't really belong there.*

Reading that got me thinking about my own personal word and whether or not it matches the word for the city in which I am currently living. Before I consider the present though, I skip briefly back into my past to acknowledge that over the years there have been different words I'd likely have used as **my** word. Words such as: innocent, curious, confused, and yes, even sex (which was Rome's word per Gilbert) was in there for a good portion of the time. Once I became a mother, nurturing would have been a word I'd have used as my own for a time. If Gilbert's theory is correct, then it's not surprising that while I lived in one city and one city only during my nurturing years, my sons and my own self were all nurtured by that city and its inhabitants during our time there.

It is also interesting to note that I moved around a great deal in my childhood and adult life. As my own life changed and my word with it, so too did the word of each city in which I found myself. My personal word may have matched in some places. I know it did not match in others. One town I lived in for a mere three weeks: no time to even get to know the word that fit that town, let alone to know if it matched my own word at that time in my life.

And now as I come to my life today, and the town in which I reside – before I let you know if there is a match between the two, I would address the city's word first. Without hesitation, when I give thought to this word, according Gilbert's theory, as it applies to the city of Victoria, British Columbia, Canada, it is simply and eloquently this: blossom. Whether used as a noun, such as a flower blossom, or as the verb to blossom, both are appropriate for this city of gardens. With the temperate climate all year round, we have flower blossoms even during the winter months when the rest of our country experiences snow and cold temperatures.

For three years prior to moving here, my husband Mike and I lived in a different part of this same province, on the mainland in the semi-arid Okanagan Valley with its mountains, deserts, and incredible lakes. As beautiful as that city and surrounding areas were, I never felt at home there. Guess my word and its word were no match one for the other.

Often over the years I was drawn to the memory of one incredible city that I saw for a mere 48 hours during a vacation back in 1986. I fell in love with that city, its gardens, its beauty and its people. I couldn't have given you a word for this place back then. I didn't have a word for myself back then either. If I were to apply a word now for the person I was back then, I'd say it was: conformist. I was someone trying to be what I thought others wanted and expected from me. In hindsight it was a sad way to live and yet, had I not had that experience, I'd not have known the sense of contrast that gave me the impetus to change. So I am truly grateful for who I was then.

Today, I live in that City of Gardens, an amazing world-renowned vacation spot – Victoria – and her word 'blossom' is indeed the very same as my own. As of this writing, I have been here a mere 16 months, yet I am immersed in her culture, her people, and her heartbeat. What a blessed experience and daily joy! My life has blossomed in ways I could not have conceived even two years ago.

Though I have always considered myself a writer, since I arrived to live on Vancouver Island and in the city of Victoria, my writing has taken on a depth and quality that has far surpassed even my own hopes and dreams. Before now I felt as though I were always a bud – yet one that had never opened to reveal its full potential and inner beauty.

I came to Victoria – the city of blossoms – to do just that: to grow and blossom into the fullness of me. The growth has been, and continues to be, incredible. The blossoms of my self are lush, plentiful and opulent.

Yes, I'd have to say that this particular theory, for me, holds truth and value. Thank you Elizabeth Gilbert for sharing this concept with us!

May I suggest, Dear Reader, that you take the time to review your own city and especially your own personal word? Is there a match for you both? Have you been restless and drawn to the travel bug for no apparent reason? Or are you content with heart, hearth and home? Does any of this resonate with you?

Chapter Seventeen

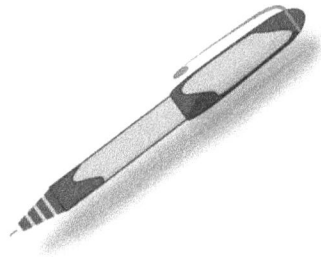

One Extreme to Another

With all of Victoria's beauty, her lovingly tended gardens, well manicured lawns, trees in profusion everywhere and her plethora of peoples from all over the globe who choose to vacation here and also to retire to this amazing city, it is with sadness that there are individuals unable to provide sufficiently for themselves and who live on the streets.

Over time, with eye contact and a simple smile to certain souls receptive to the glance of a stranger, it is possible to get to know a few of these less fortunate folks. It is to several with whom I have been blessed to share smiles that I dedicate this next poem:

**hand tanned, worn, aged, scarred
outstretched, palm up, hoping for
the touch of a coin**

Due to the more intense mood of this three line haiku, it is more commonly referred to as a senryu style (see more on specific poetic styles in Chapter 36 – April 2010 and Micropoetry).

****

In spite of the sadness of the topic, there is a delightful story to be shared here. My husband Mike and I were traveling by bus to the downtown core of the city. For whatever reason, one that I do not recall in the moment, we were each going our own separate ways with me staying on the bus to another part of town. Mike had disembarked from the bus and stood on the sidewalk back from the area where the pedestrians and passengers gathered. As the bus pulled away, he waved a farewell to me and I happily returned the gesture. I also kissed the palm of my hand and blew that kiss his way.

Between my location in the bus and Mike's location on the sidewalk, stood a sweet, older woman with all of her worldly possessions neatly organized and stacked into a grocery cart. She was facing me. She did not see Mike behind her. She only saw me waving happily and blowing her a kiss. Her face lit up with the most incredible glow and she smiled a broken-toothed grin back at me that tore at my heartstrings.

I continued to wave, yet now I was intentionally smiling and waving at the woman with the broken-toothed grin who was smiling back at me.

Chapter Eighteen

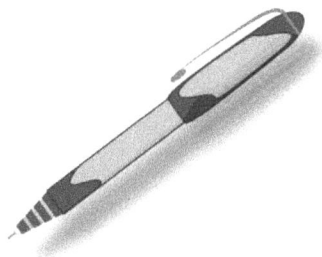

Becoming More

*N*ew-job fear surfaced with a shocking strength that had me waking up moody and broody. Was it fear of failing to make a wise choice – had I chosen the right move, taking on the role as assistant at a B&B? Or was it fear of success – that it would be a wonderful move and absolutely perfect for me? What was it I really wanted my life to look like in the months ahead? Poetry, definitely! Yet at that time I didn't see poetry as providing me the financial security that I needed.

So, what did I see as holding me back – keeping me from realizing my dreams? What actually were my dreams? What did I see as options/possibilities for me? Not having the answers in the moment (though somewhere inside me I knew that I knew the answers) meant it was time for me to write another Pantoum – such a powerful and yet simple way to reveal issues and clarity:

Becoming More

Becoming more
My personal goal
Incentive. Inspiration.
Purpose.

My personal goal
To grow.
Purpose.
To blossom.

To grow
To add to all that I am
To blossom
Into fullness and beauty.

To add to all that I am
The enrichment of life
Into fullness and beauty
Wholeness. Completion.

The enrichment of life
Incentive. Inspiration.
Wholeness. Completion.
Becoming more.

Chapter Nineteen

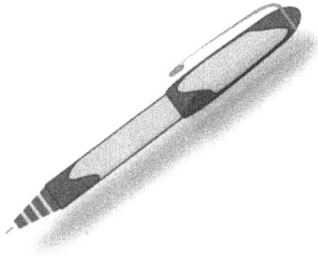

Living a Poem-Focused Life

*T*he answer to my current quandary was to become more. How did I see myself growing and becoming more of who I was? What provided me with the sense of wholeness and completion? How could incentive and inspiration translate into action within my life?

I kept coming back to poetry. Everywhere I went, everyone I met, every action I took gave me poetic opportunities to express my world in the written word. My voice in ink on paper made a statement unique to me and me alone. No one else experienced my reality. They may have been where I was, seen the people I saw, yet no two people shared the same sensations, responses, feelings, emotions and perceptions. Like snowflakes, there could never be two identical poems written about a single event, person, place or thing. Never!

So, taking Wendy Morton's idea of poeming people to a personal and professional level, could I do it? Did I have the courage? Thinking about it was one thing. Talking to people was something I did easily. I had, after all, been trained by the best to engage people in conversation. But writing poems about people from my perception and then giving them those poems ... really ... could I do it?

A voice in the depths of my being was hollering a resounding YES!

Of course, I could and did: while I was at Queenswood that was exactly what I did! Could I do it outside of the safety and confines of those hallowed halls?

Poems
Primed for presentation
To people anywhere, anytime
Spontaneously delivered
And powerfully gifted
For purposes
Only known at the level of
Instinct and inspiration

****

That same night I had a dream telling me clearly to record my stories and poetry NOW – capital letters and all! In the dream, my grandsons were asking me to read to them from Grandy's Book. I'm their Grandy. The thought to write a poetry book had been a concept off and on for a while. Yet I never took any steps toward its fulfillment. This dream and my grandchildren's faces before me touched me so deeply that I knew I had to make this possibility a very serious reality. It was then, back in late May of 2009, that I began to truly focus on making this book real in my life – to make this a dream come true.

My gift to my Grandchildren
Whether or not I meet them
Whether or not I know them
Whether or not they meet me

To let them know they are loved
They are honoured
They are cherished
They are precious

Dear Grandchildren of my heart
You have a rich heritage
Family who care about you
Who are glad you are here

You have chosen wise parents
They have chosen a powerful child
Find ways to learn and grow
From and for each other

Allow yourself to be
All you can be and more
Challenge yourself to surpass
Your own expectations

Always remember
- And if you forget –
Return to the feelings
Of always being loved.

Chapter Twenty

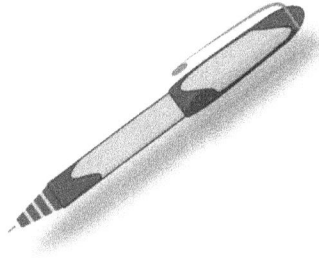

A Tool from my Teens

*I*t has always been easy for me to engage people – particularly strangers – in conversation. I learned this valuable skill from the most unexpected source – a teacher – back in my teenage years.

At the age of seventeen, I entered nurse's training fresh from high school. In those good ol' days (and I'm talking about the mid-1960s), the nursing course was three years long and was taught right within the hospital itself. I had only been in classes for one week when I went onto the actual hospital floor – in the paediatric wing – in my newly starched whites – apron, bib, collar, and cuffs – over the basic blue dress. The new, and very comfortable, white shoes with white stockings (attached by garters) finished the look, with one exception. The final touch was the pre-formed, starched white cap perched smartly atop my short-cropped brown curls.

So young an age to take on such a responsibility, I hadn't learned enough about who I was within myself to know what I wanted in a lifelong profession. Needless to say, I didn't stay past the first year of training. Yet from this one nurse – my favourite of all our teachers – I gained a world of knowledge.

The topic of the day was communication. We were to be taught how to chat up our patients in order to draw from them the information we needed to record on their charts. It was intended as a functional lesson. Here are the keys to get people talking ... ask questions; record their answers. Here is a list of types of questions to ask. A sheet of paper was given out, then, if I recall correctly. Simple: study the questions; know them – the types of responses they can be expected to generate. Functional: practice them on each other.

However, this teacher went on to tell us a story: something that had apparently happened to her. She shared it with us and it went something like this:

One day Miss Brown (sadly I do not recall her real name) was flying from her home in Toronto, Ontario to Los Angeles, California to meet with family and friends for a week's vacation at a famous beach. Her seatmate on the flight was an elderly gentleman. Miss Brown engaged him in conversation and found out that his name was (let us say potentially) Mr. Jones. She asked Mr. Jones the basic questions – what we refer to today as open-ended questions that will garner a more informed response than a mere yes or no answer – and every time he gave her an answer she took one item or noun or verb from what she heard him say and she expressed it back to him in the form of another question. Here's an example, as I remember her telling us:

Miss Brown: "Where is it that you are going today?"

Mr. Jones: "Los Angeles to see my daughter and my granddaughter."

Miss Brown (taking one word from Mr. Jones' conversation and turning it into another question): "Your granddaughter?"

Mr. Jones: "Yes. She's turning 10 tomorrow."

Miss Brown: "Ten. How delightful! Are they having a party for her?"

Mr. Jones: "Sounds like it will be a grand affair."

Miss Brown: "Grand? Grand in what way?"

Mr. Jones: "Apparently they are planning on taking her – and all of us – to Disneyland."

Miss Brown: "Disneyland. How wonderful for you all! Have you ever been there before Mr. Jones?"

Mr. Jones: "No!"

Miss Brown: "No?"

Mr. Jones: "No and I'm not interested in such nonsense, not at my age."

Miss Brown: "Your age ... you're still a spring chicken! What do you think you might want to do there?"

Mr. Jones: "Well, I really like musicals. I hear there are a few stage musicals being presented. I wonder if my daughter would mind if I go see one of them instead of the rides and such?"

Miss Brown: "I bet she might go with you, if you ask her. I'm sure your granddaughter would enjoy seeing a Disneyland musical with her grandfather! Would you like that?"

Just as the plane was descending into the Los Angeles International Airport (LAX), Mr. Jones thanked Miss Brown for the conversation.

"Miss Brown, thank you so much for the most amazing conversation! I don't think I've enjoyed myself so much in a very, very, long time!"

Not once during the entire flight did Miss Brown ever tell him anything about herself. With her skills, she was able to engage him in a one-sided chat that filled several hours.

(Note: Looking back today, I realize that the groundwork for this dynamic skill came originally through my dad's natural ability to utilize this very same method – encouraging and fueling memorable conversations. My nursing teacher taught me the technique, my dad taught me by example.)

Chapter Twenty-One

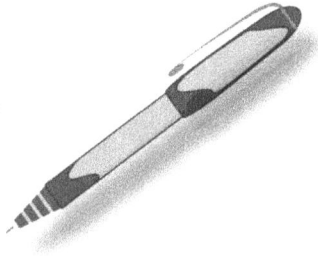

To Bus It!

*T*raveling by bus through Victoria requires advanced planning. Not to say the experience is difficult – for the most part it is quite simple and most effective. Yet the timing is critical if you have appointments to keep.

For me to get to the downtown core from my wee apartment in Saanich in the north end of the city took approximately 40 minutes from door to door. From my new location at the B&B in the Esquimalt area, west of the city, meant only a 7-minute walk to the bus stop and a 10-minute ride downtown. On those occasions when walking was the purpose of the journey and time was of little importance, it was a fabulous outing along the scenic waterside trails.

Other destinations required more time on the bus. Some routes took as much as 45 minutes one way, such as a trip west into Sooke: a small village, quaint and worth the outing. Sooke's Wiffenspit Beach is a pleasant walk along a very thin strip of land surrounded by water on 3 sides – like an isthmus. Be forewarned, though: the Spit is longer than it looks. Give yourself a good hour or more to walk the return trip!

Back to the bus: going east on the #6 bus from the B&B and then transferring downtown to a #73 bus to go north to Sidney-by-the-Sea, the journey can be an hour and twenty minutes as it makes frequent stops. By catching the #70 bus, it's like taking an express run with a much faster arrival time. It all depends upon your purpose for the trip: scenic or time constrained. All of the bus routes that go north of Elk/Beaver Lake Regional Park (another valuable worth-see location with huge lakes and nature trails) stop near the airport; then go on to Sidney and end at the ferry terminals where trips off-Island could take you to the various Gulf Islands or over to the mainland. (By the way, the bus trip all the way from Sooke, in the west, through Victoria and then north up to the Swartz Bay ferry is a mere one-way regular city fare: no extra charges at all, even though it spans a distance of at least 65 kilometres – or just over 40 miles.)

Should Sidney be your destination, it is easy to spend a pleasant day at this small touristy town of gift shops, bookstores and cafes or to saunter along the waterside walkways and out onto the newly built wooden pier.

****

For a writer, lengthy bus trips can be put to exceptional use. Carrying my writing tools with me in a convenient one-shoulder backpack, I always have ample paper and pens available. I utilized all of my traveling time well – writing about the people on the various buses – from the elderly to the infant, from students to the well-to-do here on vacation wanting to get to know the locals. Rich and poor, old and young, workers and the unemployed ... the bus provided a broad cross-section of humanity. Such is absolutely the perfect fuel for the writer's pen.

However, one day I was off on a journey to visit a new friend. I left my backpack at home and had only my purse with me. Now I assumed, incorrectly, that I would have writing materials tucked in there as well. Not so, I discovered, as a poem revealed itself to me on the longest leg of the bus trip. I scoured through every pocket, pouch and zippered compartment that bag contained – twice – all to no avail. Feeling more than frustrated at my oversight, I was about ready to use a tube of lipstick to record the details. Then I recalled that this particular purse had a wee secret location tucked away inside one of the zippered compartments. That's where I found an artist's brush pen – peacock blue – that I had purchased weeks ago. Blessings be!

Before I could even write the originally inspired poem though, this poem spoke to me first:

What is this –
A poet without a pen?
Glad tidings be
That fancy marker
Grace my person
And my purse
To allow the artistry
Of words
The creation of phrase
The lyric of tongue
To unfold in India ink
Peacock blue
Upon lined page
As yet empty
Awaiting breathlessly
The touch
Of the artist's stroke.

Chapter Twenty-Two

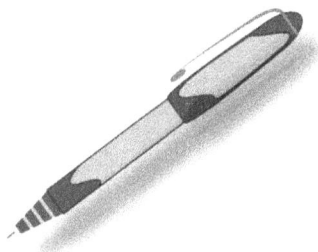

The Happy Shift

*a*s I began packing my few personal items in preparation for my move to the B&B, I found myself getting more and more excited about this next step of my journey. Another Pantoum popped into mind and I stopped midway through filling a box to write the following:

Relieved to be leaving
Ready to go
There shall be no grieving
It's time, don't you know.

Ready to go
Excited, it seems
It's time, don't you know
To follow my dreams.

Excited, it seems
To plant a wee seed
To follow my dreams
See where they lead.

To plant a wee seed
Watch for a shoot
See where they lead
How they take root.

Watch for a shoot
There shall be no grieving
How they take root
Relieved to be leaving.

When I finished writing that poem, I added the following note:

Now that was unusual. That last stanza gives (on its own) a mixed sense of grounding and rootedness, yet the desire at the same time for change ... an odd and powerful blend.

Chapter Twenty-Three

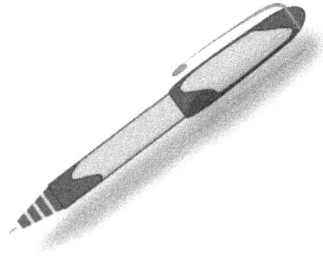

Noteworthy Quote

*W*hile all of this change was occurring in my life, I still took time to read. Reading keeps my mind sharp. Interested as I was then, and still am, in New Age or spiritual concepts, I found the following fascinating quote in **The Nature of Personal Reality – A Seth Book** by Jane Roberts:

"A flower cannot write a poem about itself. <u>You</u> can, and in so doing your own consciousness turns around about itself. It literally becomes more than it was. Existing in such diversified, rich environment – possibilities, the human psyche needed and developed a conscious mind that could make fairly concise and accurate `minute by minute` judgments and evaluations. As the conscious mind grew, now, so did the <u>range</u> of imagination. The conscious mind is a vehicle for the imagination in many ways [...] the greater its knowledge, the further the reach of imagination. In return imagination enriches consciousness reasoning and emotional experience."

Chapter Twenty-Four

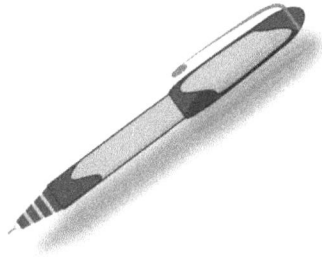

June by the Ocean

*M*aking the choice to live and work at the Bed and Breakfast over the summer was ideal. The beauty of the home, the environment in which I began living and working, the delightful woman I was working with and the incredible surroundings all provided a sense of accomplishment, peace, tranquility and even awe.

And the poetry flowed. Verse flowed non-stop from my pen, while first erupting spontaneously and profoundly from my heart.

Chapter Twenty-Five

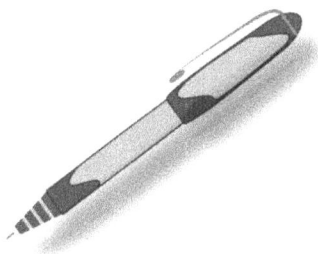

Poems and More Poems!

a massive floor-to-ceiling picture window in the living room of the B&B overlooked the Juan de Fuca Strait. On clear days the snow-capped Olympic Mountains of Washington State were visible.

When there were no guests around and the work was done for the day, I would take the time to sit at this window. One couldn't help but admire the incredible beauty. Birds, mammals, plant and marine life – all were visible from this one vantage point. It was like having a nature channel on the television – all day long!

Before coming here, I had asked for an expression of prosperity and abundance in my life – and this amazing B&B opportunity fell into my lap – totally unexpectedly and with absolutely no foreknowledge or effort on my part. I sent out blessings and such deep appreciations to the Divine for making all of this come together. The phrase (the source of which I do not recall) that the Universe conspires with me to fulfill my dreams ... is so very true!

I was in awe of the magic and the marvel of it all ... and very, very grateful ... so very grateful.

Each day was as unique as the weather, which changed constantly. And with each change came the inspiration to write what was before me – be it a bird sighting or the moodiness of a storm or any other innumerable unfolding. I wrote every moment I could.

****

Amazing Sighting

A Great Blue Heron perches upon a branch of a huge Douglas fir
Far above the roof of the home below.
The bird's mate arrives landing several branches beneath,
A female, more grey and cream.
With a lightness of being she jumps up to a higher bough:
Crunch and snuggle, time to rest.
Binoculars now removed knowing just
What lighter specks mean when seen in that tree.
In contrast to the massive wing span,
A wee hummingbird darts mere inches from my hair.

Feathered Alarm

Early risings
have me smiling
listening to my alarm clock –
the birds.

Festive greetings
they offer the day
awakening all within range
to hear.

Reflections

Reflections upon the water
Are an imperfect mirror image
Of that which is on shore
Dreaming of more.

Peace

There is calmness to the air
A peace about the water.
The blue of the sky is painter perfect
And clouds dust the atmosphere.
Hummingbirds and sparrows
Populate the gardens
Tasting every sweet nectar,
Every delectable seed and nut.
Gulls hover, scavenging.
Great Blue Herons rest and nest.
If ever there was an Eden
It was here; is here still.

Restless; waiting; impatient.
Timing is everything.
The perfection of the moment,
Now is exactly right.
Peace; acceptance; gratitude.
Everything is timed.
The moment is perfect.
Right now is exact – ideal.

Blessings Be

Special –
My connection to the Divine.

Precious –
The loving gifts provided.

Blessed –
By the bounty and the beauty.

Comforted –
Know I am supported.

Nourished –
With spiritual manna.

Loved –
As a child by its parent.

Conversations with Family

Stories told
Shared
Moments relived
Memories recalled
Vivid reflections
Laughter
Love.

Chapter Twenty-Six

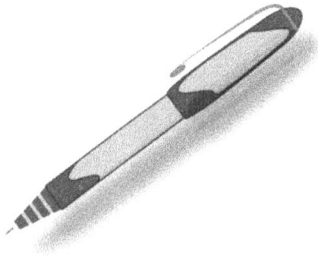

Emotional Shift

There were a few days of feeling down. It happens to me on occasion. Sometimes I have no idea what causes the shift in energy – or rather the lessening of it. Most often – as happened this time – it doesn't last long.

On one such day I found myself needing time away from my new job, from my new digs, even from the beauty of the rocks and ocean at the foot of the house. The weather seemed to sense my mood and matched my emotions with an appropriate response:

It's raining
Here in the coffee shop
From my eyes.
The droplets pour
Splashing their pain
Upon the table's surface.

I came out unprepared –
With the sunshine
Beaming its joy out to all
In the mid afternoon
When I left the house
Without my umbrella.

Chapter Twenty-Seven

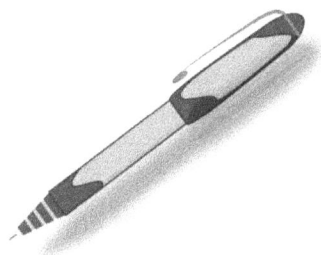

Progression through July

The wisdom of spiritualist and philosopher Eckhart Tolle and his focused attention on living in the NOW of one's life had me writing this:

Today ... in my NOW days, the simplicity of my life is becoming (notice I didn't say *already is*) enough. This is good. Merely being me ... being me breathing ... being me smiling ... being me making coffee ... being me doing dishes, sweeping, bringing in the newspaper, going for a walk, letting a little lady go ahead of me in line at the grocery store because she asked me if she could, stopping to smell the heady scent of a rose way past its beauty, yet so powerfully fragrant still ... being me writing a poem. Being me. Simple. Plain and simple. Simply wonderful.

Chapter Twenty-Eight

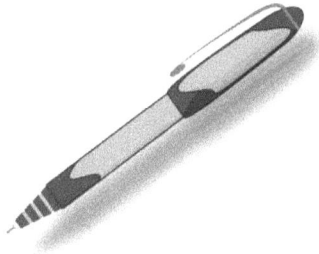

In Honour of My Mom

*Y*ou may – or may not – have noticed that there is no bus pass for the month of August 2009 in amongst all the other monthly bus passes on the back cover of this book.

The entire month of August I spent back east in Ontario with family. My mother had passed away in August of the previous year and I wanted to be near her resting place on the anniversary of her transitioning to her new life.

That month was good for me, visiting with family and friends. Reunions were planned on both sides of the family – both my father's and my mother's clans. In addition, my youngest sister's youngest child was getting married in Cape Cod. It was nice to be able to drive south into the United States to be there for that event as well.

At the end of August, as I was awaiting my flight back west to Vancouver Island and what was now my home city of Victoria, there were extensive delays. Seems there were severe thunderstorms all around the airport. No flights were allowed in or out. We were not even able to board the plane that was on the runway – as the passengers from that plane were still in their seats, not even being allowed to disembark till the lightning stopped!

This particular lightning storm seemed exceptionally memorable considering that the previous year about this time, my mother's funeral was in full swing. All of my siblings and our father were in the same limousine as we left the funeral home. The sun was shining and the day clear ... until we got near the cemetery.

My brother looked out the limo window and then expressed to us all an apology.

"It's my fault," he said. Naturally, we all asked "Why?"

Mother loved lightning; we all did thanks to her passion for powerful thunderstorms. Apparently, our brother had spoken to our mother before her passing, suggesting to her that when she transitioned, if she had any clout when she got 'there', to send us a single bolt of lightning.

With that admission, all of us looked out the limo windows – to see the dark storm-clouds gathering over the cemetery. As we left our vehicles and circled around the burial site, the skies opened up and dumped rain upon us. Everyone who may have come prepared ran to their cars to get umbrellas. The limo driver had a half dozen she grabbed for us to share.

Then, just as the minister began to speak, the lightning struck: one huge bolt. We collectively counted out the seconds till we heard the thunder. Yet before the thunder resounded in the valley, there was another bolt of lightning ... and another ... and another. We were circled by lightning strikes all around!

Standing under the broad canopy of an aged tree, the minister looked at our father, made a hand gesture of placing her right thumb and index finger only an inch apart from each other. She was saying to Dad, "Shall I keep this sermon short?" Dad nodded an affirmative.

I think that has to have been the shortest eulogy in recorded history.

As we drove out of the cemetery and back to the funeral home, we realized that it had not rained anywhere but where we were. And now, here we were, my family and I, in a funeral limousine, tears of delight and laughter streaming down our faces:

"Mom, you've not just got clout ... you've got CLOUT!"

****

To this day, when there is a thunderstorm, each of my family can be seen looking up at the skies and heard saying: "Hi Mom!"

(In honour of my mother's passing – August 10, 2008)

Thunderstorms

All around us
Accumulations of vocals
Specific emphasis
Punctuated with light,
Audible expressions
The closest communication of
My mother's love –
A tangible gift
Packaged within
Rumbling clouds,
Wrapped in amongst
The hyper-charged beauty
Of a thunderstorm.

Chapter Twenty-Nine

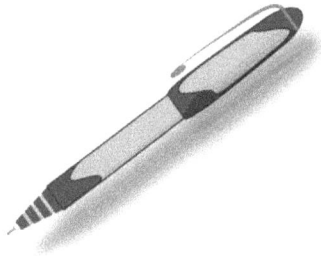

Fog Horns in September

The fog horns were in full and loud use this particular September day. The temperature inversion had created a blanket of white mist hazing anything within visual range; obliterating everything beyond a few meters.

I heard, rather than saw, the gentle lapping of incoming tidal waters. I smelled the sea kelp that normally bobbed above the shoreline surface of the Juan de Fuca Strait. Children were playing in the nearby park; their laughter arrived to touch my ears and bring a smile to my face, though I could not see them.

There was an eerie quality to the day. Most often this type of fog affected the area early in the morning; yet today it was well past noon.

The musical interlude of placement and tone of the fog horns of various ships afloat somewhere in this Brigadoon mush of cloud was a delight to the senses – all of them – and worth so much more than a mere moment of observation and enjoyment.

A poem emerged from the above prose – a drawing of words into a detailed and finite picture of my experience:

The Fog

My world as I know it is gone.
I step into the fog
To feel the moisture
Taste its freshness
Smell the aromas of both
Land and ocean scents –
Heady.

The lapping of gentle waves
Upon the rocks I know to be below
Are a soft accompaniment
To the orchestration of ships horns –
Tones and frequencies
Varying with proximity
And urgency.

Through the haze
Their call can be heard
"I am here"; "Be cautious";
"Tread slowly"; "Touch me not";
Between admonitions sent
And messages received –
Warnings.

There is a peace to the interlude:
A solitary moment of acceptable,
Appreciated aloneness.
One woman on the planet
Content in her privacy,
Breathing deeply, quietly –
Sighing, smiling.

Chapter Thirty

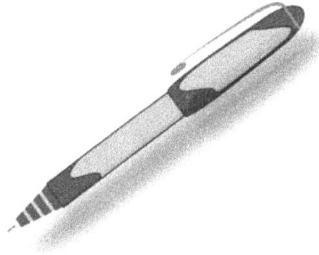

Canadian Thanksgiving

*T*hanksgiving is normally a time when I give thanks for all the blessings in my life – and to list them would fill more than a single book. Yet Thanksgiving of 2009 blew in a few challenges on the early autumn breezes.

Not one to be daunted for too long, each potential problem had its own magical resolve; the outcomes surprising everyone involved – including, or maybe especially, me!

To begin with, my position at the B&B came to an end. Though the owner had talked of extending her guest room availability into the winter months, there were not enough clients booked to warrant a live-in staff member. The final decision, logically, had to be made that I end my contract with her as originally planned – immediately following our Canadian Thanksgiving the second Sunday in October.

Just as the above decision was made, my bachelor apartment in Saanich opened up for my return. Does this surprise you? It shouldn't, as this is an example of just how magical my life is!

My husband Mike had closed up our place in Kelowna, packed all of our belongings and moved them into a heated storage unit there. He was now available to come join me here in Victoria. Perfect timing! Mike thought sweetly to stay behind in the Okanagan Valley another week in order to spend the Thanksgiving holiday weekend with his parents there and then he flew to Victoria on October 19[th.]

Now, here we were, two adults about to live in a tiny bachelor apartment just barely big enough for one. However, it didn't matter one iota: having my husband back in my arms again was so worth the closer quarters!

Yet with each unique obstacle that presented itself, and the always-positive outcome, there came little time for writing: journaling, yes. Not poetry, though. I felt as though I had stepped back to before my retreat at Queenswood and my decision to move forward with my dream of writing poetry as a purposeful, passionate endeavour.

Mike's arrival was cause for celebration, though. He had only ever been through Victoria once, as a teen, on a trip to visit friends living up-Island. There was so much here for him to see and do. I had him hiking trails starting from the city's Inner Harbour by the Legislative buildings, the Fairmont Empress Hotel and the Hotel Grand Pacific off toward Shoal Point and Fisherman's Wharf. We jaunted along by Ogden Point and on to Clover Point where he watched the kite-flying demonstrations.

There is such scenic beauty and all of it perfect fodder for Mike's camera. We walked along the shores of Cadboro and Oak Bays and more trails in and around Esquimalt starting by the Canadian Naval Base there. We hiked up Christmas Hill and Mount Douglas, and we walked along the Lagoon.

All of that walking was a very good thing indeed as we also found ourselves eating our way through the city! We had a dinner buffet at the Fairmont Empress in the world famous Bengal Lounge. We adore Indian cuisine and were pleased with the choices as well as the atmosphere. The Vietnam Garden offered award winning Vietnamese foods. Floyd's Diner became a regular haunt for us – great for fabulous breakfasts and a lunch-time treat of their bottomless bowl of homemade soup with tasty breads for dipping.

The list goes on and on! To this day we still vary our restaurant locations, trying anything and everything this fair city has in the way of dining options. Then once a month we write about our experiences in our Food category on our blog post. Do know that if we ever have an unfavourable experience (and there's not been one yet!) we will not write it up. We want the list to be only our positive experiences.

There have been journeys for us up-Island. Now, keep in mind that everything outside of Victoria, the most southerly point on Vancouver Island, is up-Island! We rent a car each time and have been as far north as Qualicum Beach, stopped into Parksville and watched the goats eat grass on the roof – yes, the roof – of the general store in the tiny little hamlet of Coombs. We have driven north and then on west out as far as you can travel on land to Tofino and Ucluelet, staying overnight at a B&B in the middle of a forest and yet just a few moments walk from Chesterman Beach at Tofino. We walked the sandy shores everywhere we went. Being there, one truly feels the power and the immensity of the Pacific Ocean.

Even as far up-Island as we got, we have barely seen a quarter of this island. I recall a visitor to Victoria asking me if they could drive to the northernmost tip and back in one day. I did all I could not to laugh ... this may be an island, yet it is 22,870 square miles or 36,800 square kilometres in size! Mike and I have much traveling yet to do in order to see it all!

As enjoyable as traveling may be, we preferred staying within the city. We found ourselves stopping in at local coffee shops in each of the small villages that make up the outer landscape that borders the downtown core – Oak Bay, Cook Street Village, Fernwood, James Bay, Cadboro Bay and more. We love our coffee and the atmosphere of local cafés is so utterly charming: each one unique and worthy of a visit.

Busy as we were back in October, Mike and I decided to step out as professional bloggers with our http://www.wolfnowl.com/ website. (And yes, Mike is the wolf and I am the owl.) We entitled it M&M's Musings and it has since built up into a varied collection of our writings, wisdoms, photography, dining experiences, being green posts and my poetry corner. In this latter category most of my better verse can be found – and much of the knowledge that I have gained in differing aspects of poetic structure.

Chapter Thirty-One

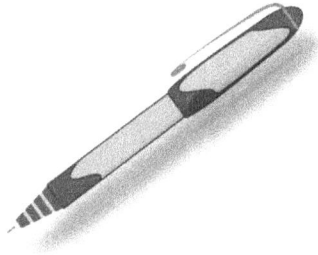

November and "Nanowrimo"

*N*ovember is National Novel Writer's Month – Nanowrimo. Done through the internet via http://www.nanowrimo.org, November became an inspired and inspiring month for me: thirty consecutive days of writing the great – in my case Canadian – novel requiring a minimum of 50,000 words. It really can be done; I proved it to myself. What an amazing month that turned out to be. Fifty-two plus thousand words and very little sleep later, I had the beginnings of a fabulous novel.

The prize, to everyone who made the limit within the time allotment, was a printed copy of their book in their very own hands and the option to sell their book on an on-demand basis through Amazon.com. What a tremendous gift to someone like myself who had not had the privilege of being published prior to this occasion.

Needless to say, November was a write-off when it came to poetry (pun intended). I had a creative outlet for my writing and I wrote copious amounts every single day! However, there were no poems to add to my collection during that month. That was now two dry months in a row.

Dry, for poetry that is, and yet tremendous in the creative aspect of my writing skill, and incredible in the re-establishing of my relationship with my husband. I'd say that made for a very lovely November.

What a joy it was showing Mike around Victoria. Everything was new to him. We bussed around town, going from village to village, and sightseeing like tourists. I watched him fall in love with the city that had become my home these past many months.

Home. Though we had only a small apartment, this city was now our home. Everywhere we went, everything we did, everyone we met ... it was like greeting a part of ourselves – for the very first time. People in Victoria are the friendliest folks you could meet: generous, caring, helpful, considerate individuals who made you feel welcome in this our corner of the world.

Chapter Thirty-Two

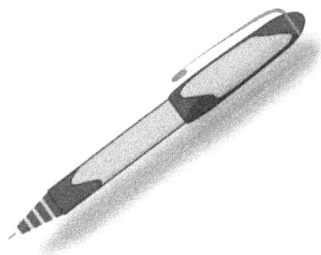

December

The month of November came and went. My novel-writing days were at an end now. It was time to begin the editing process of what I had created. Thinking that there would be extra time to focus on things other than my novel – such as my passion for poetry – I was both amazed and appalled at the amount of effort and attention to detail required to upgrade what I had recorded during those thirty days of frenetic creativity.

When I began the novel, I had my characters being and doing certain things in certain ways. By the time the last chapter had unfolded, the first chapter was no longer appropriate. Seems my characters had ideas of their own that they wanted to express. I was along merely to transcribe their tale!

Sadly, the editing became more of a burden than a pleasure. It was then I decided that for what remained of this month of December, I would let the book mellow on its own and would readdress it in the upcoming New Year of 2010.

As a result I was able to focus on my poetry. My blog's Poetry Corner took on a life of its own. In addition, I found a wide variety of the haiku-style of poetry surfacing through the internet on Twitter. My youngest son had introduced me to the Twitter world and those I began to follow either had a spiritual intent – as did I in my life – or a poetic one. Perfect for me!

I began to study and practice the haiku methods of what is referred to now as a form of micropoetry – short poems that meet Twitter's prerequisite of a maximum of 140 characters. In several of the following chapters you will discover some of the gems of knowledge about these poetic styles that I found in my research.

In addition to the shorter styles of poetry that seemed to resonate well with my naturally creative focus on life, I was still writing other longer poems that demanded and delighted my attention. Here's one in honour of the Christmas holiday, celebrated by many in Canada, and dedicated to my grandson:

Christmas is for Children

With laughter and mischief
the giggling child
ran hither and yon
darting in and out
over and under
and around
everything in his way
preventing speedy arrival
at his targeted destination –
the gaily wrapped presents
under the Christmas tree.

****

Speaking of Christmas, our very first in Victoria was filled with all the traditional sights and scents: decorations and lights, cedar boughs and hot apple cider. There was no snow: none – neither before nor after the holiday season. Yet even without the white stuff, the mood of the community was festive and happily contagious. The Santa Claus parade was well supported both by the local clubs and merchants as well as by the attendees themselves: like us, children of all ages came out to cheer on the floats and the bands and, of course, the jolly old man himself.

A wonderful surprise for me between Christmas and the New Year, was the 90-minute, horse-drawn carriage ride through the downtown core and into the oldest community of Victoria, James Bay. What a perfect ending to round out the year!

Chapter Thirty-Three

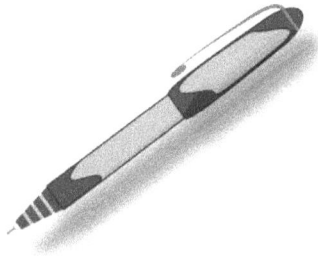

Happy New Year 2010

*Y*ears ago I bought myself a small spiral notebook and pen to keep in my purse. On the very back page of this notebook I began jotting down different topics as they came to me randomly – for use as poems, short stories, or as simple paragraphs that might, someday, find their way into a story or a verse. It's a mere list that looks somewhat like this:

Grandmother
Thunderstorm
Mashed bananas
The scent of a baby
Fresh ground/fresh brewed coffee
Candles
Riding a bicycle
Driving a car
The first pickle in the jar
A hug ...

This list fluctuates with the number of topics I still might write about – someday. Many have already inspired me to write. Some I have written about and yet I have kept the topic on the list as there are so many ways to express the different facets of that same topic – such as thunderstorms! Each and every storm is unique and pulls emotions from within as varied as the storms themselves!

How do I use this **Potential Writing List**? On days when I know I want to write, yet I am uninspired as to topic, I pull up my list, which is now in the computer. Seldom do I choose the topic immediately following the one I used last. I usually allow myself to be drawn randomly to something specific that sparks my creative passions! This topic I'll most often use as a starting point for a poem.

Why a poem? Writing poetry, for me, is a first step to connecting with my inner writer. Poetry is often a sudden burst of inspiration. Because most poems are relatively short, one can be completed in less time than it takes to prepare a meal. The resulting poem is a permanent record of my emotional, spiritual and/or physical experience of that time in my life. They are fun to re-read years later.

During this particular exercise I find it best to simply connect with the creative energy inside. Once the pen hits the paper and the words start to flow – or once the letters appear on the computer screen – thoughts and feelings begin to surface. Playfulness tends to come to the forefront of my imagination and I begin to 'see' possibilities that exist in my mind only. Utilizing expressions and creative phrases to describe events or emotions becomes a game. The more elaborate I can craft a stanza, the more fun it becomes for me!

Let me give you a 'for instance'. When my kids were little, they were restless when confined to the car on trips. Once they were of an age to imagine – and that was by the time they could string words together in sentences – I'd get them practicing their creativity. One such very long trip I had each of my sons choose an animal. My one boy chose an elephant. The other chose a mouse. Perfect! Then I had them describe their animal out loud – which they did. Then I suggested that they put clothes on their animal. And each item of clothing was to be put on them one piece at a time. Before the second piece of clothing was put on, the first piece of clothing was mentioned. Then before the third piece of clothing was added, the first and second piece of clothing was mentioned. Also, each piece of clothing had to be a different colour and put on to a different part of the body.

For example, there was a grey elephant. This grey elephant put on a pair of blue Bermuda shorts. The grey elephant put on a pair of blue Bermuda shorts and then a bright red T-shirt. The grey elephant put on a pair of blue Bermuda shorts, a bright red T-shirt and then a yellow belt to keep his shorts from falling down! Once their animal was fully dressed, then they'd have them doing crazy things. The elephant, for example, might put on roller skates and skate beside us holding on to the car door with one hand while holding the string of a kite in the other. Or the mouse would hide in the glove compartment and make noises that would make Dad think there was something wrong with his car engine! Seldom did they tire of it as they could imagine that elephant and mouse in the car with us and they were laughing and enjoying the creativity of it all.

Once the children got older and knew about rhymes, we started to create crazy poems in ways that rhymed.

One such silly poem, again on an elephant theme, was the following:

Once there was an elephant
Who tried to use the telephant.
No, no, I mean an elephone
Who tried to use the telephone!

Yes, it's a kids' exercise in creativity, but it works for us as adults as well! It works especially during those times when we are less than inspired to write, yet understand the value of consistent practicing and the honing of our writing skills. There are just some days when the destination of the completed writing is of less significance than the journey of the writing itself.

So, let's go back to the **Potential Writing List**. It doesn't take much to get started writing, once inspired. What it does take is the desire to actually take out the list and make a choice: then to sit down and write something. Anything! That takes committed action. No one can do it for you. It has to come from within you. The more you make the time to do it, the easier it becomes. The better the results you have with this, and the more you mobilize the fun aspect of the experience, the more inclined you will be to act upon it!

Random topics are what I record in the *back* of the notebook. Here's what I write in the traditional fashion, starting on the first page – all the poems, descriptive phrases and paragraphs related to those very topics!

For example, one paragraph I recorded in the wee hours of a morning:

"I awoke one hot summer night to the heart-pumping drama of thunder. Stepping out onto the tenth floor balcony of my small apartment, I watched a storm approach. Forewarned by the blaze of cloud-splitting razors of lightning, I counted the seconds between the light show and the sound I knew would soon follow. A thousand one, a thousand two: a child's way to count the seconds between the light and the ear splitting sound of the thunder to come. The climax to this incredible show that night was a spectacle never before seen and likely not to follow in my lifetime – one bolt of lightning found its target in the mechanics of a hydro substation. The resulting fireworks were far superior to any pre-planned Canada Day celebration I have ever witnessed – and I've been to some amazing fireworks demonstrations over the years."

What this is leading back to, in a round-about fashion, is that after I had allowed myself to experience the incredible moments of magic and marvel of that storm, and to feel – really feel – the awe and beauty of what had just transpired, I sat with that small notebook and I jotted down all the nouns and descriptive words and phrases that came to mind spontaneously. Many of the words I wrote that night have found their way into various poems and stories. Some of them I used in the descriptive passage above.

Over the years I have filled more notebooks than I have taken time to count – there are a few gems in each. Not everything I write is valuable. Often-times exercises and practices are just that – practices. Yet there are poems and paragraphs in those books that, when I look at them now, I find myself thinking: WoW! Did I really write that?

I've started going through those old books, pulling the jewels out from the pages and entering them into my computer. That in itself has been, and continues to be, an amazing journey.

May something here inspire you to find the **Potential Writer** in you. It's a journey well worth the first step!

Chapter Thirty-Four

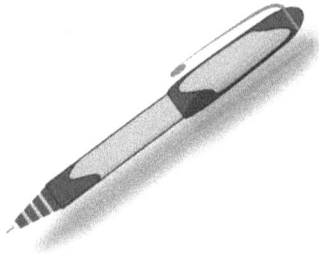

February – Origin of Words

*a*s both a poet and a writer, the origin of words is a fascinating topic. The knowledge and application of words is an essential tool for the poet. Comprehending the meaning is vital. Add to that the quality of understanding its root source and you have an edge that enhances the gift of gab and the very presentation of form and function. Put it all together and you add richness and depth to your work.

Learning about the origins of words has a classification all its own known as **Etymology**: it is the study of the origins of words.

There are other word uses that have some very strange names as well – and some pretty specific applications for those uses. See if my poetic descriptions of the individual words can give you enough of a clue to determine the definition of each:

Defining **etymology** defines its origin of use
Provides history, form and meaning
And, over time, some noticeable abuse.

Tick-tocking sounds and other suchness
When word and sound do sound alike
Then **onomatopoeia** is the word of muchness.

Philology, philologically speaking,
Gives linguistic form and meaning
To the texture of your text.

Dialectology provides direction,
And with detection,
Informs location.

Had fun with those!

Chapter Thirty-Five

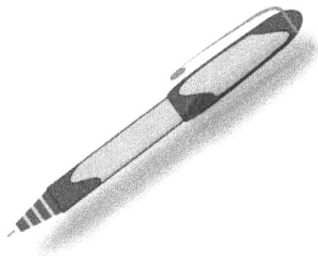

March 2010

*I*n the month of March each year, spring arrives in Canada – especially here on the southern tip of our beautiful Vancouver Island. With idyllic temperatures, our green shoots and the crocus and snowdrop flowers come into full blossom.

Blossoming once again was my poetry. The more I wrote and the more I learned, the more varied my styles and the resulting work became.

The term micropoetry was a new term for me, even as versed (pun intended!) in poetic styles as I was. Being relatively new to Twitter, I learned that the use of what is referred to as a hashtag [#] was a way to connect with people of like minds or like topics. For example, if you want to share micropoetry with others you add the phrase #micropoetry into your tweet (your Twitter message) allowing others interested in the same topic to see your poem: similarly for #haiku or other short poetry styles. This works also for finding people interested in non-poetry subjects such as #hugs or #spring or #photography.

Here are some of my more recent haiku and micropoetry:

The body slumbers / in moonlight spirit dances / sips on tears of joy.
#haiku

Tulips bloom / two lips arch / smiles blossom.
#micropoetry

Welcoming smiles / crack the landscape / of a happy face.
#micropoetry

Powdered sugar snow / dusts the lawn / sweetening the day.
#micropoetry

On the bus a child / knows all of her A B Cs / sings to me sweetly.
#haiku

****

Now this last tweet poem was done to haiku style, which means the use of three lines condensed into one line for tweeting purposes where the forward slash [/] is used to separate each line. Also the first and last lines have five syllables each, with the middle line having seven syllables.

The haiku style usually refers, somewhere within the poem, to nature or the seasons – spring, summer, etc. (though aspects of the day/night such as moonlight are also used – see my first example). In this last haiku about the child singing, I did not refer to either a season or an aspect of the day. Though not a true haiku poem, it does fall within the structural parameters.

Also the 17 syllable limitation gave me little room to truly explain the amazing interaction I had with this child. She sang her ABCs song over and over and over again. After each finale she and her mother would applaud her success. After the second round I applauded as well. This child made direct eye contact with me and on her third round she sang the song specifically to me! I smiled. She smiled. I think she was hoping I would sing along with her: after all the last line of the song is: "Next time won't you sing with me!" Sadly I didn't. But when she applauded, I applauded! The mother apparently didn't catch on, but continued to support her daughter with her own hearty applause as though it were her child's first ever performance – each and every time. As did I, I must admit!!!!

Needless to say – or rather, it is worthy of saying! – that a three line haiku poem could not fully capture the emotion and the interaction I experienced. I wanted to say more. Yet I wanted to send it out to the Twitter world. Therefore my message still needed to be kept to a maximum of 140 characters – that included all letters, numbers, punctuation and even spaces.

Formally, the final poem looked like this:

On the bus
a sweet voiced child
having learned her ABCs
repeatedly sings and sings
enticing you to join along.
Applaud. Applaud!

Here, however, is the final Tweet. It included the phrase '#micropoetry' so that it would go out to the common theme group as well as to those 280+ people (bless you!) who follow me:

On the bus / a sweet voiced child / having learned her ABCs / repeatedly sings & sings/enticing U 2 join along. / Applaud! Applaud! #micropoetry

Can you tell I am enjoying this newly discovered creative outlet?

Chapter Thirty-Six

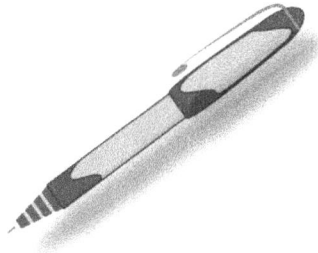

April 2010 and Micropoetry

I mentioned in Chapter 32 that I had set up a Twitter account for myself. Many of the folk who follow me are interested in an uplifting, positive and more spiritual interaction. In fact, I only follow people who are poetically focused or uplifting in their tweets.

Of those whose poetry and verse I follow, it seems that micropoetry (#micropoetry in the Twitter world) is happily becoming a new past-time. Short poems, such as haiku, senryu, tanka and now the latest called gogyohka, are all the rage.

Though I've been writing poetry for most of my life, haiku was not commonly known and was not taught in schools when I was younger. In fact all of these styles are new to me. I tend to write very little in the senryu style as it is so similar to the haiku but with a more cynical tone to it. I do not do cynical. I am a true Pollyanna and see the best in, and of, everything!

In brief, here are definitions of some of the more commonly used haiku styles of poetry:

Haiku is a Japanese lyric or verse form having three unrhymed lines of five, seven, and five syllables, traditionally invoking an aspect of nature or the seasons.

Senryu is a Japanese form of short poetry similar to haiku in construction: three lines with 17 or fewer syllables. Senryu tend to be about human foibles while haiku tend to be about nature. Senryu are often cynical or darkly humorous while haiku are more serious. Unlike haiku, senryu poems do not generally include a season word.

Tanka is a five-line style of poem with more structure and form than the gogyohka poem (see below). Tanka uses syllable structure of a 5-7-5-7-7 count and there is a pivotal middle, or third, line in the poem.

Gogyohka is a relatively new form of Japanese short poetry, founded and pioneered by Japanese poet Enta Kusakabe. Gogyohka is pronounced **go-gee-yoh-kuh** (the "g"s are hard as in "good"), and literally means "five line poem". Gogyohka is five lines of free verse on any subject matter. There is no set syllable pattern; however the poem should be short and succinct. The goal is to capture an idea, observation, feeling, memory, or experience in just a few words. Thinking of each line and taking a single breath to speak it gives the poem a sense of sensuality rather than a cadenced structure.

I have written several dozen or more short poems the past few months, since I discovered the simple and personal enjoyment that I receive from this easy, natural process. I thought to give you a highlight of a few of my favourites from those I've written most recently – with the first group being primarily haiku and a few senryu:

Brush strokes of sunset / paint the soul with radiance / the heart with pure joy

Box of bright crayons / colouring book lays open / my inner child smiles

My heart is smiling / my nose and toes are tingling / laughter fills me up

Fishes fast swim by / schools of thought to teach the young / gathering to feed

Love a new journal / blank pages allow fresh new / concepts for haiku

Teddy bears sitting / on chairs waiting for people / to cuddle and hug

Rainbow lollipops / plate-sized decadence to lick / sweetness into life

Deep breath draws to me / scents of summer fragrance lush / exhales winter thaw

Ancient tree canopy / late afternoon leaf shadows / stretch out across time

194

Here's one that started off as a micropoem – short in length but not of 17 syllables:

Petals grace the ground, having first graced the flower, then the air as they fell.

Replacing one of the two-syllable words (flower) with a single syllable word (plant), and moving the placement of the word "then", it became a haiku: (line one – 5 syllables, line two – 7 syllables, then line three – 5 syllables). I've included the haiku version for you here:

Petals grace the ground / having first graced the plant then / the air as they fell.

Through Twitter, many of us who write micropoetry have recently become inspired with a more extended style of haiku – known as gogyohka.

Gogyohka is a fun and easy form of verse, making poetry writing accessible to everyone, including children. Yet it is challenging as a method of practice for self-reflection, contemplation, and the distilling of one's thoughts.

Though the tanka also adds the two extra lines for length and additional content, it is the gogyohka style now that I tend to favour when there is more I want to say than the standard haiku style. And there is one more wonderful aspect of the gogyohka style that delights me ... I don't have to be counting out syllables on my fingers in public!!!! Most of my inspiration comes from public outings – at malls, coffee shops, on buses. I often wonder what strangers are thinking when they see me counting with my fingers ... and especially when they can't see what it is I'm counting!

For me, using the extended five lines with no syllable count, merely one gentle breath per line, expands the potential of poetry options.

Let's go back for a moment to the variances between styles with an exercise:

Here's a visual for you: picture this – a tall, slim man, wearing a denim jacket and jeans, a black T-shirt, runners, a black and purple head band around his forehead holding back his long salt & pepper hair, with a full beard and moustache. It is Summer time. You see a child pointing at this man and saying something softly as he points. The child is excited! As you get closer to the boy you hear what he is saying. The child's father is pulling the boy's hand to get him to move quicker – seems the dad is anxious to be off to another errand and is not paying attention to his son.

This is what I wrote in haiku style: 3 lines with 17 syllables, 5-7-5:

Santa in summer
denim, headband and T-shirt
child's voice HO HO HO

(Yes, that's really what the child was saying! Children just *know* these things!!!)

But there was more I wanted to convey than the basic facts so I went to the more expanded version of the gogyohka style by breathing in the *feelings* of the experience!

Santa
in summer garb
of denim jeans and T
still, a child's small voice
HO HO HO

Then I thought to add more detail to see if it enhanced the visual while delving a wee bit deeper into the emotion through the breath:

Santa in summer
denim jacket and jeans
T-shirt and headband
still, small child points
HO HO HO

Looking at them all, sounding them out, the breath effect is best with the second of the three. That's the one I liked most and tweeted that day!

****

Here are a few other gogyohka poems I've written recently:

sixteen:
a gangly age
desiring grace
exemplifying beauty
tripping on a leaf

happiness smiles
relaxing muscles
lighting eyes
infectious
rewarding

gentle rain nourishes
body and soul
cleansing, releasing
freeing up the old
making way for the new

the arrow
slides forward with
speed and alacrity
striking its target
cleanly

public speaking
terrifies the most ardent
of orators
knocking knees and sweaty palms
hidden

spring Sunday
store doors open
coatless patrons wander
within, without, about
contentedly

sunset symphony
scents of cedar
and fresh mown grass
titillate the senses.
I'm smiling!

skipping rope
in full swing
dancer inside
the arc of
enthusiasm

****

I originally wrote the following as a #sixwords poem – the simple use
of six words as a complete statement or phrase, regardless of the
number of syllables in each word:

Shore, shell, stone, driftwood ~ blended beauty

I converted this to a gogyohka style when I found myself *breathing* the
poem, especially the last line, each time I spoke it in my heart:

shore,
shell,
stone,
driftwood –
blended beauty

Chapter Thirty-Seven

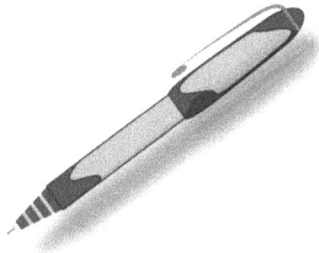

May 2010 – Poetry as Play

*I*n doing some research on poetry to add to the scope of this book from your perspective – as a reader – the number of poets who come into this medium with a heavy heart is disheartening.

Poetry needn't be dark, painful, gloomy and morbid. It can also be such fun! Take any topic. Add humour. Rhyme or no rhyme, matters not. Put sentences together that match, or mix lines up a bit for added flavour.

One afternoon when my eldest son was four and a half years old, he wandered out from doing his thing in the bathroom and his trousers were down around his ankles. Here's the poem that surfaced in my mind and onto the page:

Oh little boy at half past four
with trousers dragging on the floor
the bathroom may now be a chore
yet every day I love you more.

No topic is too simple or foolish or too often written about by others to be written about by you if you are inspired to do so from a creative and playful bent. If you find magic in the world around you, anything and everything can be your inspiration!

Do you watch the clouds and 'see' pictures in them? This has been a family pastime since I was a girl and I instilled it in my sons as well. My husband Mike is a photographer and sees faces in clouds, on rocks – everywhere he goes! The following is a poem inspired by one such gathering of clouds:

White clouds growing
changing in the east
building, expanding as though
the Ghostbuster's Marshmallow Man
was very slowly arising
stretching up and out
from a long held crouch.

Here's an exercise for you if you're so inspired to indulge:

Below I'm going to give you the description of someone I saw one day last summer. I would encourage you to write a poem – or several poems if inclined – about this individual. Be playful. Be inventive. Trust the words that come to your mind. Write them down no matter how foolish!

Don't edit what words you hear in your head before you write them out, and don't edit them once they're on the page. Never use an eraser! Never use the delete key! Once words have been removed, you can't get those thoughts and inspirations back. And trust me, some of my worst phrases or sentences may have been inappropriate for the piece I was working on at the time, yet – lo and behold – I found them to be modifiable and ideal for something else along the way!

Here's the description:

> *An 80 something woman with long ringletted hair, wearing a sun-faded yellow, broad-brimmed hat with wilted blue silk flowers. She sports an aged gingham print summer dress hiked to her knees, showing off her rolled-down support hose while riding a rust-red bicycle. She hums a tune that has her smiling. Though you do not recognize the tune, imagine it to be ... any tune you choose. Possibly: K-K-K-Katie, Beautiful Katie, You're the only G-G-G-Girl that I adore ... Or maybe: Barney Google, with the goo-goo-googly eyes, Barney Google with a wife who's twice his size ...*

(yes, those really were songs that were popular in her day!)

Now, may I suggest you make a poem from the description on the previous page as it inspires you. Make it playful, fanciful, light, loving. Yes, you can make it sad if you are so moved … yet my hope for your expansion here would be to show you how easy it can be to become poetic – in every aspect of your life, from the frying pan's sizzle to the awe of dew drops on the first crocuses of spring – and to do it playfully as a child might.

Here are a few examples from my own inspiration:

The yellow hat brim flapped and flapped
Against her cheek it slapped and slapped
The bicycle chain it tapped and tapped
As the old woman hummed a tune.

Or how about?

The blue flower wilted, drooping sadly
Rolled support hose retracting badly
Little old lady peddling madly
Humming gladly.

Or this one?

Yellow hat and wilted flower
Hair in ringlets a winded mess
Support hose rolled beneath the knees
Above the knees a gingham dress.

I'll leave you now with, hopefully, inspirations floating around in your own mind. Go find that pen and some paper, open up your word processor, or be brave and use the white space here in this very book! Whichever method you choose to use, have fun with it!

Happy poeming!!!!!

Chapter Thirty-Eight

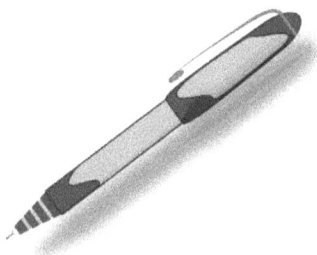

Poem or Poet?

*W*hat do you think of when someone mentions poetry? Love? Longing? Beauty? Pain? And yes, even humour – particularly if you think of limericks:

There once was a man from Turmeric
Who liked his stew spicy and very thick
He sprinkled in some hot pepper, then more
Took a swallow, then swore
What he said can't be used in a limerick.

The use of words is the storyteller's and the poet's craft. The tools of the trade are a writing instrument and a source on which to write. No expensive purchases or overhead costs are needed. The heart, the brain and a skilled ability to utilize language is fundamentally all that is required. That's it.

A storyteller uses his or her skills to weave a tale that captures the reader/listener and holds them spellbound till the final word. Description and storyline are essential. Believable characters are mandatory. Dialogue is optional. There is a beginning, most often a climax and then an ending to each story.

A poet has two options: to tell a brief story using the same structure as the storyteller, but in fewer words; or to take one descriptive element – what would be a paragraph to a storyteller – and grant it the grace of standing alone.

Thomas Hardy (1840-1928) was an English novelist and poet – one of my very favourites. For me, Hardy brought description to life. In his book **Return of the Native**, Hardy used descriptive phrases that captured all of the senses to hold the reader in a particular place, a specific space, a powerful feeling during the entire reading of that one paragraph. His tangible crafting of art through language lifts the black letters from the cream/white page, adds colour and dimension, texture and taste. Each sense is heightened to a palpable degree of reality in the moment. And when the last word or phrase of each paragraph has been read, the sensual pleasure remains like the savouring of a pure dark chocolate long after the confection has melted.

Hardy's writings were all dark and brooding (forgive me Thomas if you wrote anything light hearted, for I have not yet had the privilege of experiencing it). It is not so much his storyline and characters that appeal to me – it is his innate ability to craft pictures and feelings with words.

To me, a good writer has the ability, skill and talent to write prose or poetry that allows the paragraph or phrase to stand alone – solid, sure, stately and with grace.

A poet's gift is even more than that: being able to turn a thought, emotion, picture, or phrase into a stand-alone unit that includes not merely words but also an underlying pleasure of music as well. The fluid grace and flow, the balance and symmetry, the rhythm and cadence add harmonics without instruments; overtones that resonate in the soul of the reader/listener. A poet is a short story teller accompanied by an amazing orchestra!

For those of you reading these words who feel that you are not, and could never be, a poet – you may appreciate the following quote that I received recently via a Twitter tweet:

> **"If you cannot be a poet, be the poem."**
>
> **- David Carradine**

A well-written poem helps you to see what the eyes do not perceive, to taste what is not touching your tongue, to smell what is not inspiring your nose, to hear what is not brushing your ears, to feel what is not caressing your skin.

So if it is not in your nature to bring these senses to life through words, may I send out a request to the Universe on your behalf that you be blessed with the ability to live all of those senses to the fullest expression in every aspect of your day's experiences? Allow all of your senses to be heightened and be fully aware of them all – each and every one. Live life totally. Get into mischief. Smile to the depths of your being. Cry from your soul. Whisper your passion so softly the person next to you cannot hear it with their ears yet feels it with their spirit. Sing from your heart. Dance like a child. Love as much, as often and as deeply as you want to be loved – with no expectation of its return – yet rejoice fully when it is reciprocated. Should you undertake to do this you will find yourself living large – being the very epitome of the fully aware, strong, powerful, multi-dimensional spiritual being that you are at the core and depth of your unique and beautiful individuality.

In the expression of each moment of your day – your life – you will be able to feel and to know your ability to stand tall, strong and on your own. With the loving hand of the Divine, God, Source, the Universe, All That Is happily recording the description of you in the history of time and space as you reveal your life in this three dimensional reality – *you become the poem*.

Chapter Thirty-Nine

The Last Journal Entry

*S*eems appropriate on this very last day – Day 365 – of A Year in the Life of this particular Bus-Traveling Poet that I would have the following horoscope:

Sagittarius: You are about to undergo a radical change in your outlook; the kind of change that happens only two or three times in a life span. What is your number one creative ambition? Make that the focus of your existence.

Wow! Such an incredible statement – a validation, if you will – to both honour and cement the very aspect of my initial request back when I started this year's journey – to find answers, to know my purpose. Here, then, is my last journal entry of this year from May 2009 to May 2010:

My number one creative ambition is, and has always been, to be a professional poet. To make this the very focus of my existence thrills me immensely. My vibrational frequency is piqued, at peak potential merely in the thinking of such a possibility – to live every day for, with, through and to my poetic skills. Such joy fills me. Smiles surface from the deepest aspects of my being to lighten my heart and lift the corners of my mouth. My eyes twinkle with the marvellous and mischievous anticipation of this unfolding.

To take myself to places I am inspired to be, moment by moment, grants me the blessing of living my life through trust and inspiration. Knowing that in each moment I am where I am meant to be: interacting with co-creators; utilizing and gifting my skills and talents in ways that express who I truly am – how I connect with and contribute to others – bliss!

Being me – fully, unequivocally, indubitably, profoundly, purely me. Blessings be!

I breathe poetry...

yet

it also breathes me ...

THE END ?

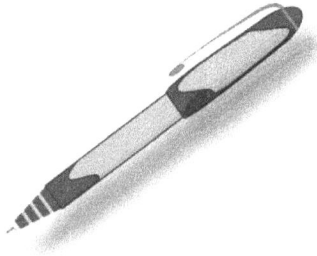

Definitely not!

For me ...

this is just the beginning ....

Dedication to Queenswood

Merely one week prior to the printing of this book, I sadly received the following through my FaceBook and Twitter connections:

June 17, 2010

Dear Queenswood guests, supporters and neighbours,

It is with great sadness that we share the news that Queenswood retreat centre will close permanently on October 1st, 2010.

As you may know, Queenswood has been in operation for over 40 years, and it has always been subsidized by the Sisters of St. Ann. The Queenswood Society for Spiritual Growth was established in 2004 to assume the management of the retreat centre and help Queenswood continue its service to the community as a long-term legacy of the Sisters of St. Ann. On January 1, 2008, the Sisters of St. Ann and Queenswood Society entered into a 3-year agreement with the hope that Queenswood would achieve financial sustainability independent of the continuing subsidy from the Sisters by the end of December 2010.

In March 2010, the Sisters of St. Ann announced the sale of their Arbutus Road property to the University of Victoria (UVic). It was hoped that Queenswood might continue its operations as a tenant of the university. Negotiations for a lease with UVic proceeded with good will, but with the best terms possible, capital and operational expenses would require fundraising a minimum of $3.5 million over the next five years in order to fund a 10-year lease, capital costs and operations. We were advised by fundraising experts that this target is not feasible. Therefore, last week the Queenswood board of directors recommended the orderly closure of Queenswood.

Further updates on the closure of Queenswood will be posted on the Queenswood website at www.QueenswoodVictoria.ca/closure,

including ways for the Queenswood community to come together before the closure.

We wanted to let you know personally about this decision, which will be announced in the news today. Meanwhile, we hope you will consider taking a summer workshop or retreat to enjoy Queenswood one last time. Descriptions of our summer programs are available online at:
http://www.QueenswoodVictoria.ca/summer.

Thank you for your support and prayers.

Sincerely yours ...

******

Dear Reader,

My heart aches to know of this. I am, however, immensely pleased that I had chosen to write my book at this time, as an honouring, if you will, of all that Queenswood is, and what it has been, to the incredible community of Victoria, British Columbia, Canada.

Marcia

217

Marcia Mae Nelson Pedde lives life large with her husband Mike in the north end of Victoria on Vancouver Island in the province of British Columbia, Canada. Marcia's sons, Chris and Nick, her daughter-in-law Vanessa and (at the time of this publication) her two grandsons also reside in British Columbia, in the city of Vancouver, on the mainland – a mere ferry ride across the breathtakingly beautiful Strait of Georgia.

Originally from Ontario, Marcia still has extended family back east. Acknowledgements and love go out to her father, Robert Charles Nelson, and her siblings Carol Nelson, Pamela Kotzeff and Brad Nelson, all of whom – in addition to Marcia's husband Mike and sons – are her greatest and most ardent and inspiring supporters.

Follow Marcia on Twitter at http://twitter.com/tomarciamae/ plus check out both Marcia and Mike online at http://www.wolfnowl.com/

The incredible **COVER ART,** including the back cover photo of a Blue Flag Iris and the above photo, was craftily conceived and digitally designed and created by Mike Nelson Pedde – with the deepest appreciations from his loving wife.

(The above picture was taken atop Christmas Hill, the highest peak of the Swan Lake/Christmas Hill Nature Sanctuary north of Victoria.)